# CAKES
## AND PASTRIES COOKBOOK

Good Cook's Library

# CAKES
# AND PASTRIES COOKBOOK

Annette Wolter

**Crescent Books**
New York

# Contents

# About This Book

People who bake are creative, and enjoy pampering themselves and others with home baked goods. The quality of the final product is also an important argument in favor of home baking. One knows what is in the dough which is another reason for the continued use and enjoyment of fine baking cookbooks.

The luscious results of each recipe are shown in the color pictures made specially for this book. In addition, the pictures offer lots of suggestions for enticing garnishes and decorations, and for attractive ways of serving cakes, pies and cookies.

Of course it was not easy choosing the recipes. This cookbook offers a rich mixture of favorite, well-known as well as exciting new cakes and pies in various adaptations, both traditional and modern recipes. These cakes and tarts taste good, are easy to make, and will please those who are looking for something special.

The recipes are simple and easy-to-follow, and of course, conscientiously tested. As an additional help the basic types of dough are presented step by step in picture and text. These clearly show how yeast dough is prepared as well as the rules for making sponge cake, meringue, butter cake, rich tart pastry, Danish pastry and others. The descriptions and pictures are clear enough that even the novice will be encouraged to experiment. Also find helpful tips on work methods.

There are notes for each recipe on the time it takes to prepare it and how easy or difficult it is to make. Special notes also indicate whether the recipes are famous, or regional specialties, or whether they are particularly nourishing. The information on preparation and baking times, as well as the time it takes to complete the dessert makes it possible to plan ahead.

There are four main chapters. First indulge in "Cakes and Tarts made with Fresh Fruit." They taste best with local fruit in season. But of course use exotic fruits too, of which there is such a rich choice available, and often at very reasonable prices. Uncooked fruit is rich in nutrients that is why uncooked fruit is often placed on a prebaked cake, or arranged on a delicate custard, garnished with jelly, cream, meringue, almond slivers, etc. In the more traditional recipes the fruit is baked with the cake. Besides several apple cakes, included is at least one cake or tart for almost any kind of fruit. The big advantage of cakes with fruit is that the fruits can often be used according to whim, season or taste.

The second chapter treats "Baking Pan Cakes." Of course there are the stars, like streusel cake, savarin, cheesecake, fruit cake and stollen, also included are a lot of lesser known cakes that offer tasteful surprises.

The subject of the third chapter is "Favorite Cookies and Pastries." These include the most varied possible cross-section, like favorite croissants, doughnuts, pastry pockets, squares and bars, cupcakes and jelly rolls. Discover many new items with which to enlarge ones repertoire.

The best comes last with "Festive Cakes, Tortes and Tarts" in the fourth chapter. They are all worthy to crown a festive occasion. Even their appearance is seductive. But have no fear, these are not the complicated products of professional bakeries. With some care, patience and attention to detail, any cook will be able to make all the cakes in this chapter, even without specialized training or knowledge. The tortes are so enticing one will want to pretend the calories are not there from time to time.

Before starting to bake, and even before shopping for ingredients, read the "Tips on Method." Here useful points on successful baking can be found that are not included in the individual recipes.

Enjoy choosing from these recipes and have fun baking.

# Tips on Method

Baking is an exercise in creativity. But in order to be really successful, and for results that are a pleasure to eat, one has to be precise, and pay attention to a few basic rules. Read the following points carefully, and recall them when baking.

All ingredients must be measured out exactly. Measurements in tablespoons (tbs.), teaspoons (tsp.), and cups indicate leveled off spoons and cups, unless otherwise indicated. The measurements for liqueurs are given in tablespoons.

Ingredients should be laid out, preferably already measured, about 30 minutes before beginning work, so that they will be room temperature. This is especially important when making yeast dough. Pie dough is an exception; it needs to be cold. Start with hard butter and cut it into pieces with very cold hands and knead it quickly into the other ingredients. For meringues, too, the egg white should come straight from the refrigerator.

In most cases butter is recommended for shortening. Of course, margarine can also be used.

Yeast doughs and rich tart pastries especially can use an additional pinch of salt to bring out the flavor. For these doughs try using salted butter whereas it is recommended that unsalted butter be used in all other recipes.

When using the rind of citrus fruit look for untreated products if available. Otherwise carefully wash any citrus fruit with lukewarm water, as they have all been sprayed with a thin layer of wax to protect them against injury during transport.

Only very brief descriptions were possible in some cases. Because of this some of

the more frequently recurring procedures were abbreviated whenever necessary. The step-by-step instructions in the general information section of the book where various types of dough are described, supplement the recipes with some very useful material.

Before rolling out rich tart pastry or yeast dough in the desired form, dust the work surface lightly with flour. It is also a good idea to rub flour on the rolling pin to keep the dough from sticking to it. Be careful not to add too much flour as the quality of the dough will be distorted.

As flour is an important variable in the success of these recipes, please take note of the following rules: for baking cakes and pastries a light, airy flour is required, such as sifted cake flour; for deep-fried tarts and pastries, all-purpose flour is recommended; unbleached flour or all-purpose flour is recommended for baking all cookies; a flour high in gluten is necessary for breads, for example whole-wheat flour or bread flour. Throughout this book the single word "flour" is used. As described here, the appropriate type of flour should be applied to each recipe unless a specific flour is already given.

Yeast dough and tart pastry, both with a low fat content, along with cheese-and-oil dough and strudel dough should be baked on a greased jelly roll pan or in a greased baking pan; butter cakes, pound cakes and sponge cakes require a greased and floured sheet or pan, or dust with ground nuts, crumbs, sugar, etc. For layer cakes made with sponge cake batter, only the bottom of the pan should be greased and floured. The ungreased sides ensure that the cake rises evenly and prevent it from slipping back down. With jelly rolls, meringues and macaroons the jelly roll pan should be lined with parchment or waxed paper. First it is best to grease the pan somewhat so that the paper does not slip. For cream puff dough, rich tart pastry and puff pastry the jelly roll pan is untreated, aside from rinsing it with cold water for puff pastry.

For flat and low cakes like cakes made with fresh fruit, baking pan cakes, layer cakes, croissants, yeast braids and loaf or low tube pan cakes, the middle rack of the oven should be used. High cakes like Gugelhupf or Pannettone belong on the lower rack.

The test for doneness makes it absolutely clear whether the cake is baked through. For flat cakes simply go by the color of the surface, which should be yellow to golden brown. For cakes baked in tube pans, stollens, yeast braids and loaves, test the cake by inserting a toothpick into its highest point; if it comes out clean the cake is done. If not, it needs to bake another 5 to 10 minutes. To prevent an already brown cake from turning black if further baking is needed, cover it with parchment or waxed paper. Turn off the oven and let the cake "rest" in the oven another 5 to 10 minutes.

If the cake has burned in spite of all efforts there is a trick to save it: rub the burned side with a grater and cover it well with icing.

Cakes and fresh dough can usually be frozen without any problem. To retain the fresh taste of the cake it is best to freeze it when it is still somewhat warm in freezer paper or freezer bags. When taken out, wait until it has thawed before topping it with fresh fruit or glazing it with icing.

# Types of Batter and Dough

## Sponge Cake

This aromatic and foamy mixture made of eggs, sugar and flour can hardly be described as batter. The eggs can be worked in either whole or separately; by either method the batter is beaten so long that the air bubbles that form clearly enlarge the volume of the batter. Ground hazelnuts, walnuts or almonds are folded into the batter with the flour. Fine Madeira cakes are made in the same way, with the addition of cooled melted butter. It is important to preheat the oven well ahead of time, to avoid making the sponge cake batter wait, as it collapses easily.

Butter only the bottom of a springform pan and sprinkle it with cake or bread crumbs. Preheat the oven to 350°. Carefully separate 6 fresh eggs. Beat the egg yolks with ¾ cup plus 1 tablespoon sugar, ½ teaspoon vanilla and 2 teaspoons warm water or orange juice until they are light and foamy.

## Jelly Roll

Jelly rolls are a snap. In the simplest version spread heated apricot jam on the still warm cake, which is then rolled up, and dusted with powdered sugar. To fill the cake with whipped cream mixed with fruit puree, butter cream or cream cheese, place the warm cake on a damp kitchen towel, remove the parchment or waxed paper and allow the cake to cool under a second damp towel. According to the filling the jelly roll can be imaginatively decorated. In the recipe section of the book (pages 80 and 81) suggestions for other delicate fillings can be found.

Make a sponge cake batter out of 8 egg yolks, ⅔ cup sugar, a pinch of salt, ½ teaspoon vanilla, 4 egg whites and ⅓ cup plus 1 tablespoon flour, ⅓ cup cornstarch and ⅓ cup cocoa. Spread it out on a jelly roll sheet (jelly roll pan with edges) lined with parchment or waxed paper and place on the top rack of the oven, preheated to 425°. Bake 8 to 10 minutes.

## Meringue

Meringue is nothing more than dried egg white into which a good deal of sugar has been incorporated. With ingredients like instant coffee, finely grated chocolate and ground nuts, the taste of meringues can be varied. Meringue can be made into delicate cookies, pressed from a pastry bag with a large rosette onto a jelly roll pan lined with parchment or waxed paper; or tart shells filled with fruit and cream; or tort bottoms, pressed through a simple pastry bag onto the jelly roll pan in a spiral beginning at the center. Meringues without special ingredients can be made to keep in stock. They must be kept dry.

Using an electric beater whip 1 cup egg whites (from about 8 eggs), with a pinch of baking powder until fluffy. There should be no trace of yolk in the egg whites, and no trace of shortening in the bowl. Very gradually add 1¼ cups plus 1 tablespoon sugar with the beater on the lowest speed; then turn to the highest speed and beat until stiff.

## Fritter Batter

Simple fritter batter is like a rather thick pancake batter. Dip apple rings or pieces of day-old white bread filled with plum marinade in the batter and fry them in hot oil until they are golden brown on both sides. Oils that are good for deep frying are neutral vegetable oil, shortening and coconut oil, which are completely water free and do not smoke or burn at high temperatures. In frying, the temperature should be between 325° and 375°.

Whip until stiff ¾ cup whipping cream with a pinch of salt. Mix in 2 eggs. Stir in 2 cups less 1 tablespoon flour, cover and set aside 1 hour.

With a clean whisk or a rinsed-off egg-beater whip the egg whites with 1 pinch of salt until they are almost stiff. Gradually add ⅓ cup plus 2 tablespoons sugar and whip them until they can be cut. Slide the egg whites onto the beaten yolks. Combine 1 cup sifted cake flour with ½ cup cornstarch over the eggs and fold them in.

Fill a prepared pan with the sponge cake batter, spread evenly and bake 30 minutes in the preheated oven. Never open the door of the oven during the first 15 minutes of baking!

Turn the sponge cake out onto a damp towel and pull off the paper. Cover with another damp towel and allow to cool.

Prepare a simple fresh cheese or butter cream. Sprinkle the cake with Cointreau, spread it with the cream, and roll it up. Cover the roll with more cream and decorate it with rosettes pressed from a pastry bag. Garnish them with bits of orange or mandarin orange slices.

Mix ¾ cup plus 2 tablespoons sugar with 3 tablespoons cornstarch, sift onto the egg whites and fold in with a spatula. Cover two jelly roll pans with parchment or waxed paper. Preheat the oven to 200°. Fill a pastry bag with the meringue mixture and press the desired shapes onto the jelly roll pans.

Dry the meringues in the oven 2 to 6 hours according to their size, leaving the oven open a crack by placing a wooden spoon handle in the oven door. Dip the finished meringues in liquid glazing and allow them to dry. Fill with whipped cream, ice cream or fruit.

Heat 4 cups oil or 2 lbs. shortening or coconut oil in a deep-fryer or a heavy-bottomed saucepan. The temperature can be measured though somewhat less accurately by inserting the handle of a wooden spoon in the oil. If bubbles form rapidly around the handle the oil is probably hot enough.

Dip the prepared ingredients in the fritter batter (stirred just before), and fry them a few at a time in the hot oil, for several minutes on each side. Lift them out with a slotted spoon, drain and serve.

# Types of Batter and Dough

## Butter and Pound Cakes

With this kind of batter all the ingredients must be combined into a homogeneous mass through a rather lengthy process of steady beating. According to the instructions given in old recipes, the butter, sugar and eggs are to be beaten at least 30 minutes and sometimes even 1 hour, and only in one direction. Today very fine sugar is used so the time spent beating is reduced to 10 to 20 minutes. For especially tender butter cakes the eggs are worked in separately and the egg whites whipped until stiff. If less butter and sugar are used than that called for in the basic recipe, add 2 teaspoons baking powder.

Preheat the oven to 350°. Butter a tube pan and sprinkle it with bread crumbs or sponge cake crumbs. Separate 4 eggs. Whip the egg whites until fluffy. Very gradually add ⅓ cup plus 2 tablespoons sugar and whip the eggs until stiff.

## Rich Tart Pastry

Tart pastry is quick and easy to make. It needs only to be chilled for some time after it is made. Although sugar can be one of the main ingredients there is also a salty version with possibilities that are endless. It can be a crust for hearty fillings, flaky cheese pastry, the base for a cake or tort made with fresh fruit, delicate pastry or Christmas cookies. There is a standard formula for the proportions in sweet tart pastry: 1-2-3, where 1 part is sugar, 2 parts are shortening and 3 parts are flour, by weight. Eggs and liquid are not necessary, though they can be added.

Pour 2¾ cups sifted cake flour onto a work surface. Make a well in the middle, drop in 1 egg and around the edges of the well sprinkle with ⅓ cup plus 2 tablespoons sugar and a pinch of salt. Cut ¼ cup butter into small pieces and distribute them over the flour.

## Cheese-and-Oil Dough

This is a quick and uncomplicated kind of dough which, because of its neutral flavor and workability can be used in many different ways. It can easily be sweetened for fruit tortes and pastries with various fillings, as in apple pockets and raisin snails. It is as tasty in the shape of a nut-filled braid as it is forming the base for a pizza with a hearty topping. Pastry made with this dough is best eaten on the day it is made, and it tastes best fresh from the oven.

Mix 3 cups flour with 2 teaspoons baking powder, sift onto a work surface and make a well in the center. Pour 6 tablespoons of a neutrally flavored oil, 5 tablespoons milk, ⅓ cup of sugar and ½ teaspoon vanilla into the well. Mix well, and add ½ cup of ricotta or cottage cheese, a tablespoon at a time. Knead the dough well.

## Choux Pastry

Eclairs, cream puffs, and profiteroles are all made of the same unflavored pastry, a curiosity because of the fact that it is cooked before being baked or fried. Because cream puff dough is usually not sweetened it can be used either for sweet or salted fillings. The dough is soft and sticky, and is usually pressed onto the jelly roll pan through a pastry bag, or placed there in large spoonfuls. Cream puffs and eclairs should be cut open immediately after baking to release the air inside.

Briefly cook ½ cup water with ¼ cup butter in a saucepan. Remove from the heat and add 2 cups flour. Stir the dough over low heat until it comes away from the sides of the pan.

Cream ¾ cup butter with ⅔ cup sugar, ½ teaspoon vanilla and a pinch of salt until the sugar is completely dissolved. Little by little beat in the egg yolks, 3¾ cups sifted cake flour, a tablespoon at a time, and 4 tablespoons rum or arrack.

Fold in the egg whites. Fill the tube pan with the batter and place on the middle rack of the preheated oven. Bake 50 to 60 minutes. Toward the end of the baking time test the cake with a toothpick or small wooden skewer. When it is done turn the oven off and allow the cake to sit 10 minutes inside the oven.

With very cold hands quickly knead the ingredients together into a smooth dough, shape it into a ball, cover and chill 30 minutes to 1 hour.

Set the dough on a lightly floured surface, sprinkle it with a little flour and roll it out. Do not work too much flour into the dough because this will alter its quality. Line a pie pan with the dough and cut off the excess. Bake 20 minutes until golden brown in a 400° oven.

On a floured surface roll out the smooth dough ¼-inch thick. With a jar cut out 4-inch circles. On each circle place a small mound of already prepared apple filling. Brush the edges with water. Fold over the dough and press the edges together with a fork.

Place the apple pockets on a pre-greased jelly roll pan and bake 20 minutes in a 400° oven on the middle rack until golden brown. Brush them with powdered sugar.

Put the dough in a mixing bowl and add 4 eggs one at a time using the bread hook of an electric mixer. After adding the first egg let the dough cool off a few minutes. With the last egg add a large pinch of baking powder. The dough will become golden yellow, smooth and shiny.

Fill a pastry bag with the dough and press wreaths onto a jelly roll pan. Bake the pastries 20 minutes in an oven preheated to 425°. Do not under any circumstances open the door during this time. Before beginning to bake throw ½ cup of water onto the floor of the oven to "create vapors."

# Types of Batter and Dough

## Yeast Dough

Yeast dough is not especially difficult to make, just be patient and allow it some time, so the living yeast cells, in combination with warmth and moisture, can multiply undisturbed. The rising time in the most common form of yeast dough is divided into three stages. According to the "cold" method all ingredients are added at once, after which the dough is covered and chilled for 12 hours. In the following example a yeast braid made of whole-wheat flour is prepared according to the cold method.

Add 1½ teaspoons dry yeast into ½ cup lukewarm milk and stir to dissolve it. Beat until foamy ½ cup softened butter with 3 egg yolks, 5 tablespoons maple syrup and a pinch of salt. Add 1 teaspoon grated lemon rind alternately with 3¾ cups plus 1 tablespoon whole-wheat flour. Mix in the yeast and milk.

## Yeast Sponge

The basic assumption when making a yeast sponge is that all the ingredients are at room temperature. Therefore they should all be measured out 30 minutes before being combined. The yeast must be really fresh for the yeast organisms to develop evenly as the dough rises. When using dry yeast dividing the rising time into three stages is useless, since all ingredients are combined at once. Connoisseurs still prefer pastry made with fresh yeast since the slightly sour flavor is more pronounced than in pastry made with dry yeast.

Pour 3¾ cups plus 1 tablespoon flour into a bowl and add 1½ teaspoons dry yeast over it. Sprinkle 1 teaspoon of sugar over the yeast, add ½ cup lukewarm milk and mix the yeast, sugar and milk with a little of the flour. Sprinkle with some flour. Cover and leave in a warm place for 15 to 30 minutes to form the "sponge."

## Danish Pastry

The basis for Danish pastry is a cold dough to which is added a large quantity of butter, as in puff pastry. A slab of butter rolled out with some flour is incorporated into the yeast dough in a number of "turns." The result is worth the effort. From Danish pastry, crisp and flaky croissants can be made with various fillings, apple and fresh cheese pockets or "snails" with nut filling, sumptuous pastries that taste best, as does yeast dough, hot off the jelly roll pan.

Dissolve 1½ teaspoons dry yeast in a scant 1 cup milk. Combine with 3¾ cups plus 1 tablespoon flour, ¼ cup softened butter, a pinch of salt, ⅓ cup plus 2 tablespoons sugar and 2 eggs. Cover and chill 3 hours.

## Turns

Turns are the secret of tender, delicate Danish pastry with the special taste of yeast dough and fresh butter. The method is the same as for puff pastry. The dough is folded over in 3 turns, chilled 20 minutes each time, and rolled out again. For particularly flaky pastry make it in 4 turns.

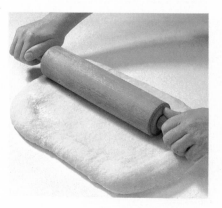

Thoroughly knead the dough again and roll it out on a floured surface to a 10 x 12-inch rectangle. Place the prepared slab of butter (which should be about the consistency of the dough) in the center, brush the edges of the dough with water and fold them over the butter.

Briefly and thoroughly knead this fairly soft dough, cover and set in a cool place overnight to rise, no longer than 12 hours. It will have doubled in volume and be somewhat firmer. Knead in ½ cup rum-soaked raisins and ¼ cup candied citron. Allow the dough to rise briefly one more time.

On a floured surface roll the dough into 3 or 4 long strips and braid them. Place the braid on a greased jelly roll pan and brush with a mixture of egg yolk and milk, beaten together. Sprinkle with sliced almonds and place it in a cold oven. Preheat the oven to 400° and bake 40 to 50 minutes on the middle rack.

Sprinkle ¼ cup butter in pieces, ⅓ cup plus 2 tablespoons sugar, a pinch of salt and ½ teaspoon vanilla around the inside edge of the bowl and combine with the yeast and milk mixture. Knead to a smooth, silky consistency. Cover and allow to rise 30 to 60 minutes, until the dough has doubled in volume.

Thoroughly knead the dough once more and roll out on a floured surface. Line a greased baking pan with the dough and cover with apple slices, raisins or chopped hazelnuts and cinnamon sugar and allow to rise another 15 minutes. Bake 30 to 40 minutes in an oven preheated to 400°.

For the slab of butter knead 1 pound of butter with ⅓ cup plus 1 tablespoon flour and shape it into a 4 x 5-inch block. Knead the yeast dough once more and roll it out to a 10 x 12-inch rectangle.

Wrap the slab of butter, in the yeast dough; then roll it out and chill 20 minutes. This process is called the first "turn."

Roll the dough out to a 10 x 12-inch rectangle, taking care to roll only from left to right and from top to bottom. Fold ⅔ of the dough together and the remaining ⅓ over them. Chill 20 minutes. Repeat the process twice.

Set the dough out at room temperature for a few minutes and work it into shapes as desired. For example, cut it into 6-inch strips, cut narrow triangles from these and roll them into croissants. Brush the dough with beaten egg yolk and bake 15 minutes in an oven preheated to 425°.

# Garnishing and Decorating

## Chocolate Icing

To make decorations with chocolate, spread melted chocolate on a greased work surface and when it is cool, shave it into little rolls. Or dip rose leaves in the melted chocolate and pull them off as soon as the chocolate has become firm.

**1** Heat apricot marmalade over low heat, stirring constantly, and brush it onto the cake. The marmalade can be thinned with 1 tablespoon of water.

**2** Knead 2½ ounces marzipan with ¾ cup powdered sugar. Roll it out to a thin sheet and lay it over the cake with the aid of the rolling pin.

**3** Cut up the chocolate, melt it over hot water, cool and heat to 90°. Use it to coat the cake.

**4** Score the cake, pressing lightly through the chocolate and marzipan layers then allow the chocolate to harden. This prevents the chocolate glaze from cracking.

## Butter Cream Garnishes

Butter cream and whipped cream are both good for pastry-tube decorations made with the writing tip or flower tip. A festive cake should never be without its delicate mounds or bold garlands of cream.

**1** Cover the cake with butter cream and coat the sides with chopped hazelnuts, toasted sliced almonds or chocolate shavings.

**2** In the middle of the cake cut out a circle with the aid of a round cutter. Fill with chopped hazelnuts, almonds or chocolate shavings to match the sides.

**3** Fill a pastry bag with the remaining cream and pipe strips, garlands, rosettes or mounds on the cake.

**4** According to the cake's filling decorate the top with whole hazelnuts, candied fruit or coffee beans.

# Decorative Sugar Icing

For a powdered sugar icing stir 1 lb. powdered sugar with 1 egg white, a little lemon juice or rum and food coloring as desired.

**1** Glaze the entire cake with the thick white icing, smoothing the surface with a spatula. Allow the icing to harden somewhat.

**2** To the remaining icing add more powdered sugar and cocoa powder or food coloring. Partially fill a plastic bag or a waxed paper cone with the icing.

**3** Cut off a tiny tip of the bag or paper and write on the cake, or decorate it with icing ornaments.

**4** Garnish the cake with silver or gold pearls, candied violets or marzipan blossoms, either commercial or homemade.

# "Dry" Decorations

Cakes, either plain or frosted, can be dusted with cocoa powder and powdered sugar. With a little imagination impressive designs can be created. Patterns made with paper stencils and sifted powdered sugar and cocoa powder look appealing and are less difficult to create.

**1** Lay ½-inch wide strips of paper on the cake in a lattice design. Sift powdered sugar heavily over the cake, then carefully remove the paper strips.

**2** Cover the cake with sifted cocoa powder. Lay a paper doily on top and sift powdered sugar over the cake. Remove the doily.

**3** On a cake frosted with vanilla butter cream lay any paper ornament. Sift cocoa powder over it and remove the paper.

**4** Sift a heavy layer of powdered sugar over the cake. Lay a paper cut-out over the powdered sugar and sift cocoa powder over that. Carefully lift the cut-out.

# Cakes and Tarts made with Fresh Fruit

## French Apple Cake

**A regional specialty, easy to make**

Preparation time: 45 minutes
Baking time: 1 hour

Ingredients for a 12-inch springform pan

⅓ cup softened butter

1 cup sugar

½ tbs. vanilla

Pinch of salt

4 eggs

¾ cup plus 1 tbs. flour

3 tbs. cornstarch

1 tsp. baking powder

1¾ lbs. tart apples

½ cup plus 2 tbs. crème fraîche

1 tbs. powdered sugar

Cream the butter with ⅔ cup sugar, ½ teaspoon vanilla and the salt. Gradually beat in 2 eggs. Mix the flour with the cornstarch and baking powder, and stir into the batter. • Peel and core the apples, and cut into slices ¼ inch thick. • Preheat the oven to 350°. • Pat the dough into the lightly buttered pan and spread evenly. Press the apples gently into the batter in a continuous, overlapping spiral. • Bake 35 minutes on the lower rack of the oven. • Beat the crème fraîche with the remaining eggs, remaining sugar and vanilla. Pour over the apple cake and bake another 25 minutes on the middle rack of the oven. • When cool, sprinkle the powdered sugar over the cake through a sieve.

## Apple-Cheese Cake

**Somewhat difficult**

Preparation time: 1½ hours
Baking time: 75 minutes

Ingredients for a 10-inch springform pan

For the pastry dough:

2 cups flour

⅔ cup sugar

Pinch of salt

½ cup chilled butter

For the topping:

2 cups ricotta or cottage cheese

1 package vanilla pudding mix

⅔ cup sugar

3 eggs

¾ cup whipping cream

⅓ cup raisins

1 lb. apples

Knead the flour with the sugar, salt, butter, and 2-3 tablespoons ice-cold water. Refrigerate the dough 1 hour. • Drain the fresh cheese, and mix with the pudding mix and sugar. Separate the eggs. In separate bowls, beat the egg whites and the whipping cream until stiff. Stir the egg yolks and the raisins into the cheese and fold in the egg whites and whipped cream. • Quarter, peel, and slice the apples. • Preheat the oven to 350°. • Roll two-thirds of the pastry dough into a circle and lay it on the bottom of the lightly buttered pan. Form sides from the remaining dough. Prick the dough well with a fork. • Spoon in the cheese mixture, spread evenly, and cover with the apple slices. • Bake the cake 1 hour and 15 minutes on the lower rack of the oven.

## Apple Cake with Rose-Hip Jam

**Nutritious**

Preparation time: 1½ hours
Baking time: 30 minutes

| Ingredients for 1 jelly roll pan |
| --- |
| 3 cups plus 1 tbs. whole-wheat flour |
| ⅓ cup flour |
| Grated rind of 1½ lemons |
| 1½ tsp. dry yeast |
| 4 tbs. honey |
| ½ cup lukewarm milk |
| 3 tbs. oil |
| 4 eggs |
| 2 lbs. tart apples |
| ¾ lb. rose-hip jam |
| ¾ cup whipping cream |
| Juice of 1 lemon |
| 2 cups sliced almonds |

**M**ix the whole-wheat flour with ½ of the other flour and ½ of the lemon rind. Add the yeast in the center and mix with 2 tablespoons of the honey, the milk and some of the flour. Set aside 15 minutes to form the sponge. • Knead the oil, 1 egg and the yeast sponge with the flour and allow to rise 30 minutes. • Quarter, peel and core the apples and slice thinly. • Separate the remaining eggs. Beat the egg whites until fluffy but not stiff. Beat the egg yolks with the remaining honey, lemon rind and flour, the cream and lemon juice. Fold in the egg whites. • Roll out the dough onto a jelly roll pan and allow it to rise 15 minutes. • Preheat the oven to 400°. • Cover the dough with apple slices, spread with rose-hip jam and sprinkle with sliced almonds. • Bake the cake 30 minutes, then turn off the heat and leave in the oven 10 minutes.

## Apple Cake with a Marzipan Lattice

**Nutritious**

Preparation time: 1 hour
Baking time: 30 minutes

| Ingredients for 1 jelly roll pan |
| --- |
| 1¾ cups blanched almonds |
| 1 cup honey |
| 2 tbs. rose water |
| 3 eggs |
| 3 cups whole-wheat flour |
| 1 tsp. baking powder |
| 1 cup plus 2 tbs. butter |
| 4 lbs. tart apples |
| ⅓ cup unrefined cane sugar |
| ½ tsp. cinnamon |
| 5 drops almond extract |

**T**o make the marzipan grind the almonds very fine in a food processor. In a pan set in hot water stir ½ cup of the honey with the almonds and rose water. • Separate 2 eggs. Knead the flour with the baking powder, 1 cup less 1 tablespoon butter, the remaining honey and the egg yolks. Chill the dough. • Peel, quarter, core and thinly slice the apples. Melt the remaining butter in a large pan, add the sugar, cinnamon and apples, cover and cook 10 minutes over low heat, stirring frequently. • Preheat the oven to 400°. • Roll out the dough, lay it on a jelly roll pan and bake 10 minutes on the top rack of the oven. • Stir the almond extract and the egg into the marzipan mixture, beat the egg whites until stiff and fold in. • Cover the dough with the apple slices. Put the marzipan mixture in a pastry bag and pipe a lattice design over the apples. Bake 20 minutes.

## Apple Pie

### Somewhat difficult

Preparation time: 1¼ hours
Baking time: 45 minutes

| Ingredients for 1 pie, or a 10-inch fruit torte pan |
| --- |
| 2 cups flour |
| ⅔ cup butter |
| 2 tbs. sugar |
| Pinch of salt |
| 1½ lbs. tart apples |
| 1 lemon |
| 2 tbs. candied ginger |
| 1 tsp. cinnamon |
| 3 tbs. sugar |
| 1 tbs. cornstarch |
| 3 tbs. apricot jam |

Knead the flour with the butter cut into pieces, the sugar and salt. Add 2-3 tablespoons water to make a firm, smooth dough. Cover and chill 1 hour. • Quarter, peel, core and thinly slice the apples. Wash the lemon in warm water, dry it, grate the rind into the apples and add the lemon juice. Chop the ginger, mix with the cinnamon, sugar and cornstarch and combine with the apples. • Preheat the oven to 400°. • Divide the dough into one slightly larger and one slightly smaller portion. Roll out the larger portion, line a pan with it and prick the bottom well with a fork. Cut off excess dough and brush the edge with cold water. Fill it with the apples. Roll out the remaining dough, set it on the apples and press the edges together, making a wavy edge between thumb and forefinger. From the remaining dough cut out shapes, brush them with water and decorate the pie with them. Cut out a hole to allow the steam to escape. • Bake the pie 45 minutes, until golden brown. • Glaze the pie with the heated apricot jam.

## Northern Apple Cake

**Nutritious**

Preparation time: 45 minutes
Baking time: 30 minutes

Ingredients for an 11-inch springform pan

1½ cups plus 1 tbs. whole-wheat flour

¾ cup plus 1 tbs. buckwheat flour

2 tsp. baking powder

¼ cup cinnamon

¼ cup ground vanilla bean

1 cup unrefined cane sugar

½ cup softened butter

½ cup crème fraîche

3 eggs

1¾ cups ground hazelnuts

2 tbs. rum

6 medium-sized tart apples

⅔ cup sour cream

**M**ix the flours with the baking powder, 2 pinches cinnamon and vanilla bean and ⅓ cup plus 2 tablespoons of the sugar. Knead with the butter, 6 tablespoons of the crème fraîche and 1 egg. Chill 30 minutes. • Toast the hazelnuts and remove the skins. Coarsely grate the nuts and mix with 2 tablespoons of the sugar, 1 tablespoon of the rum and the remaining crème fraîche. • Halve, peel and core the apples and fill them with the nut mixture. • For the custard whisk the sour cream with the remaining eggs, rum, sugar, cinnamon and vanilla. • Preheat the oven to 400°. • Grease the pan. spread the dough on the bottom, and form 1-inch sides. Add the apples with the cut side down and pour in the custard. Bake 30 minutes until golden brown.

## Swiss Apple Cake

**Easy to make**

Preparation time: 45 minutes
Baking time: 1 hour

Ingredients for a 10-inch springform pan

1¾ cups chopped hazelnuts

4 tbs. sugar

⅓ cup raisins

⅓ cup currants

3 tbs. rum

1½ lbs. tart apples

1 cup fresh bread crumbs

Grated rind of 1 lemon

1 tsp. cinnamon

Generous pinch cloves

Generous pinch cardamom

Generous pinch ginger

½ cup softened butter

⅓ cup plus 2 tbs. super fine sugar

1 tsp. vanilla

2 eggs

¾ cup plus 1 tbs. flour

⅓ cup cornstarch

1 tsp. baking powder

**L**ine the pan with aluminum foil and generously butter the bottom. Mix the nuts with the sugar and sprinkle on the buttered aluminum foil. • Wash the raisins and currants in hot water and soak in the rum. Peel and coarsely grate the apples. Mix with the bread crumbs, spices and the rum-soaked fruit. Spread over the nuts. • Preheat the oven to 350°. • Beat the butter well with the sugar, vanilla and eggs. Mix in the flour, cornstarch and baking powder. Spread over the apple mixture and bake 1 hour. • Allow the cake to cool somewhat before removing from the pan. Pull off the aluminum foil.

## Apple Tart with Almonds

**Requires some time**

Preparation time: 1¼ hours
Baking time: 45 minutes

Ingredients for a 10-inch springform pan

1¼ cups flour

½ tsp. baking powder

⅓ cup sugar

1 egg yolk

Pinch of salt

½ cup chilled butter

1½ lbs. tart apples

2 tbs. lemon juice

1½ cups milk

1 package vanilla pudding mix

2 tbs. sugar

½ heaping cup lingonberry jam

⅓ cup slivered almonds

3 tbs. apricot marmalade

Knead the flour with the baking powder, sugar, egg yolk, salt and butter. Cover and chill the dough 1 hour. • Halve, peel and core the apples and make several cuts into them. Sprinkle with lemon juice. • Make a pudding from the milk, pudding mix and sugar. • Roll out the dough, lay it in a springform pan and shape 1-inch sides. Preheat the oven to 400°. • Bake the pastry 10 minutes. • Spread the crust with lingonberry jam, then with vanilla pudding. Set the apples in the pudding and bake 35 minutes. • Toast the almond slivers in a dry pan until golden brown. Heat the apricot marmalade, rub through a sieve and spread on the apples. Scatter slivered almonds over the tart.

## Filled Apple Cake

**Requires some time**

Preparation time: 1¼ hours
Baking time: 1 hour

Ingredients for a 9-inch springform pan

1¾ cups ground hazelnuts

3 cups plus 1 tbs. flour

1 cup plus 2 tbs. butter

1¼ cups plus 1 tbs. sugar

1½ tsp. vanilla

Pinch of salt

2 egg yolks

⅔ cup raisins

4 tbs. rum

1½ lbs. tart apples

1 scant cup toasted sliced almonds

⅔ cup powdered sugar

3 tbs. apple brandy

Quickly knead a rich tart pastry from the ground hazelnuts, flour, butter, 1 cup sugar, ½ tsp. vanilla, the salt and egg yolks. Chill 1 hour. • Wash the raisins in hot water and soak in the rum. Quarter, peel, core and dice the apples. Combine with the remaining vanilla, sugar, ¾ cup of the almonds and the raisins. • Preheat the oven to 400°. • Divide the dough into a slightly larger and a slightly smaller portion. Roll out both portions. Line the lightly buttered pan with the larger sheet of pastry and fill with the apples. Cover with the other sheet of pastry and press the edges together. • Bake 1 hour. • Stir the powdered sugar with the apple brandy. • Brush the cake with the glaze and sprinkle with the remaining almonds.

## Polish Apple Sheet Cake

**A regional specialty, somewhat difficult**

Preparation time: 1¼ hours
Baking time: 40 minutes

| Ingredients for 1 jelly roll pan |
| --- |
| ¾ cup plus 2 tbs. softened butter |
| 1½ cups sugar |
| 1 vanilla bean |
| 3 eggs |
| 4 tbs. milk |
| 1¾ cups flour |
| ⅓ cup cornstarch |
| 2 tsp. baking powder |
| ⅓ cup raisins |
| ⅓ cup currants |
| 3 tbs. rum |
| 1½ lbs. tart apples |
| ½ lemon |
| ½ tsp. cinnamon |
| Generous pinch of cloves |
| 1¼ cups chopped almonds |

Cream the butter with ⅔ cup of the sugar. Separate the eggs. Cut the vanilla bean in half and scrape out the soft seed mass. Mix half of it with the egg yolks and milk and add to the first mixture. Mix the flour with the cornstarch and baking powder and fold it into the batter a tablespoon at a time. • Wash the raisins and currants in hot water, pat dry and soak in the rum. Quarter, peel, core and thinly slice the apple. Wash the lemon in warm water and grate the rind into the apples. Squeeze the lemon and mix the juice, the rum-soaked fruit, spices and ⅓ cup of the sugar with the apples. • Preheat the oven to 400°. Generously butter a jelly roll pan. • Spread the batter over the jelly roll pan and top with the apple mixture. Bake 25 minutes on the middle rack of the oven. • Beat the egg whites until stiff with the remaining sugar and vanilla seed. Fold in the almonds. Spread on the apple cake and bake 20 more minutes on the bottom rack of the oven.

## Pear Cake

**Easy to make**

Preparation time: 40 minutes
Baking time: 45 minutes

| Ingredients for 1 jelly roll pan |
| --- |
| 4 lbs. ripe pears |
| 1 cup water |
| 4 tbs. lemon juice |
| 1 cup plus 2 tbs. butter |
| 1¼ cups plus 1 tbs. sugar |
| Pinch of salt |
| 4 eggs |
| Scant ½ cup milk |
| 2⅓ cups whole-wheat flour |
| 3 tsp. baking powder |
| 2 tbs. cocoa |
| 3½ cups ground hazelnuts |
| 1 scant cup apricot jam |
| 1 tbs. apricot brandy |
| 2 tbs. chopped pistachios |

Quarter, peel and core the pears and cut into ¼-inch slices. Mix the water with the lemon juice and pour over the pears. • Cream the butter with the sugar, salt, eggs, milk, flour, baking powder, cocoa and nuts. • Preheat the oven to 400°. Butter the jelly roll pan, line with the batter and spread smooth. Drain the pear slices well on a kitchen towel (the juice can be lightly sweetened and drunk). Lay them in overlapping rows on the batter. • Bake 45 minutes on the middle rack of the oven. • Rub the apricot jam through a sieve into a saucepan, mix it with the brandy and heat. • Brush the cake with the jam and sprinkle with the pistachio nuts.

## Rhubarb Cake with Almonds

**Inexpensive and quick to make**

Preparation time: 20 minutes
Chilling time: 30 minutes
Baking time: 40 minutes

| Ingredients for 1 jelly roll pan |
| --- |
| 2⅓ cups flour |
| ⅔ cup ground almonds |
| 1 tsp. baking powder |
| 1 cup sugar |
| Pinch of salt |
| ½ tsp. vanilla |
| ¾ cup plus 2 tbs. butter |
| 2 eggs |
| 2 lbs. rhubarb |
| ⅔ cup sliced almonds |
| ⅓ cup plus 2 tbs. sugar |

Mix the flour with the almonds, baking powder, sugar, salt and vanilla. Add the butter cut into flakes and the eggs and knead with the dough hook of a mixer into a smooth dough. Shape into a ball and chill 30 minutes. • Clean the rhubarb, removing the ends of the stalks. Remove the strings and cut into 2-inch pieces. • Preheat the oven to 400°. Butter the jelly roll pan. • On a lightly floured surface roll out the dough, spread it on the jelly roll pan and cover with the rhubarb. • Bake 30 minutes on the middle rack of the oven. Sprinkle with the almonds and sugar and bake 10 more minutes. • Allow the cake to cool and cut into 20 pieces with a knife dipped in lukewarm water.

# Rhubarb-Streusel Cake

**Requires some time**

Preparation time: 1½ hours
Baking time: 40 minutes

Ingredients for 1 jelly roll pan

For the dough:

3¾ cups plus 1 tbs. flour
1½ tsp. dry yeast
⅔ cup sugar
1 cup milk
½ cup butter
Pinch of salt
1 tsp. grated lemon rind
1 egg

For the topping:

3 lbs. rhubarb
1½ cups sugar

For the streusel:

2⅓ cups flour
1 cup sugar
½ tsp. vanilla
Pinch of salt
Generous pinch of cinnamon
⅔ cup butter

For sprinkling:

⅔ cup hazelnuts
1 cup fresh bread crumbs

**S**ift the flour into a bowl. Crumble the yeast over it and stir with 1 teaspoon of the sugar, ½ cup milk and some of the flour. Cover and set aside 20 minutes for the sponge to form. • Melt the butter and mix with the remaining milk and sugar, the salt, lemon rind and egg. • Cut the ends from the rhubarb stalks and pull off the strings. Cut into 1-inch pieces, cook with the sugar and 4 tablespoons water for 10 minutes and cool in a sieve. • Knead the yeast sponge with the flour and the butter-milk mixture. Set aside to rise 30 minutes. • For the streusel, mix all the flour but 1 tablespoon with the sugar, vanilla, salt and cinnamon. Melt the butter, pour it over the flour and sugar and crumble together. Sprinkle the remaining flour over it and shake the bowl. • Butter the jelly roll pan. Roll the dough out in the pan, sprinkle with the nuts and crumbs, cover with the rhubarb and top with the streusel. Set aside another 10 minutes to rise. • Preheat the oven to 400°. • Bake the cake 40 minutes or until golden brown.

# Sunken Rhubarb Cake

**Nutritious, quick to make**

Preparation time: 25 minutes
Baking time: 30 minutes

Ingredients for 1 jelly roll pan

3¾ cups plus 1 tbs. flour
1 tsp. baking powder
Grated rind of 1 lemon
1⅓ cups butter
1 cup honey
6 eggs
1¾ cups sliced almonds
1½ lbs. rhubarb

**M**ix the flour with the baking powder and the lemon rind. Cream the butter with the honey and stir in the eggs and the flour. • Preheat the oven to 400°. • Spread the batter out in a baking pan and sprinkle with almonds. • Clean the rhubarb, cut into 2-inch pieces, lay out on the dough and press in somewhat. • Bake the cake 30 minutes.

## Berry Tart

**Easy to make**

Preparation time: 45 minutes
Baking time: 25 minutes

Ingredients for a 9-inch fruit tart pan

2 cups flour

Generous pinch of baking powder

1 egg

⅓ cup plus 2 tbs. sugar

Pinch of salt

½ cup plus 1 tbs. butter

¼ cup almond paste

½ cup powdered sugar

½ lb. strawberries

6 oz. raspberries

¼ lb. blackberries

¼ lb. red currants

¼ lb. black currants

2 packages unflavored gelatin (¼ oz. each)

1 cup red fruit juice

1 cup water

¼ cup sugar

**K**nead the flour with the baking powder, egg, sugar, salt and butter cut into flakes. Chill 30 minutes. • Knead the almond paste with ⅓ cup powdered sugar and roll out on the remaining powdered sugar to the size of the pan. • Wash all the berries and drain. Halve the larger strawberries and pull the currants from their stems. Mix the fruits. • Preheat the oven to 400°. • Roll out the dough. Use it to line the pan and prick the bottom well with a fork. Cut off excess dough. Bake the tart pastry 25 minutes until light brown. When cooled, set on a cake platter. Lay the sheet of almond paste inside the pie shell and spread the fruit on top. • From the remaining ingredients prepare a glaze, pour over the fruit and allow to stiffen.

## Rhubarb Cake with Almond Meringue

**Easy to make, inexpensive**

Preparation time: 30 minutes
Baking time: 45 minutes

Ingredients for a 10-inch springform pan

⅔ cup softened butter

¾ cup sugar

½ tsp. vanilla

5 eggs

1¼ cups flour

⅓ cup cornstarch

1½ tsp. baking powder

1⅓ lbs. rhubarb

Pinch of salt

1 cup plus 1 tbs. sugar

⅔ cup ground almonds

1 tbs. lemon juice

**C**ream the butter with the sugar and vanilla. Separate 3 eggs and blend the yolks with the butter. Mix the flour with the cornstarch and baking powder and fold into the butter and sugar. • Preheat the oven to 350°. Butter the pan. • Wash the rhubarb, cut off the ends and remove the strings. Cut into 2-inch pieces. • Pour the batter into the pan. Spread the rhubarb on top, pressing it gently into the batter. Bake 25 minutes on the middle rack of the oven. • Beat the egg whites until fluffy but not stiff. Dribble in the sugar and whip until stiff. Fold in the ground almonds and lemon juice. • Put the egg whites in a pastry bag and pipe onto the cake, or spread on with a spatula. • Bake the cake 20 more minutes.

## One-Layer Currant Cake

### Easy to make

Preparation time: 45 minutes
Baking time: 45 minutes

| Ingredients for 1 jelly roll pan |
| --- |
| 2 lbs. red currants |
| ¾ cup plus 2 tbs. softened butter |
| 1½ cups sugar |
| Grated rind of ½ lemon |
| 1¾ cups flour |
| ¾ cup plus 3 tbs. cornstarch |
| 2 tsp. baking powder |
| 5 eggs |
| 1 tsp. vanilla |
| 2 tbs. powdered sugar |

**W**ash the currants, drain on a kitchen towel and remove the stems. • Cream the butter with 1 cup of the sugar and the lemon rind. Mix 1½ cups plus 1 tablespoon of the flour with ⅔ of the cornstarch and the baking powder. Add 3 of the eggs and the dry ingredients alternately by tablespoons to the butter and sugar. • Preheat the oven to 400°. Generously butter the jelly roll pan. Pour in the batter and spread smooth. Scatter the currants over the surface. Bake 30 minutes on the middle rack of the oven. • Separate the remaining eggs. Beat the egg whites until very stiff. Beat the yolks with the remaining sugar and vanilla. Mix the remaining cornstarch and flour and fold with the egg whites into the yolks. • Spread the sponge cake batter over the cake and bake 15 minutes more. • Sift the powdered sugar over the cooled cake and cut into 20 pieces.

## Chocolate Currant Cake

### Easy to make

Preparation time: 1 hour
Baking time: 40 minutes

| Ingredients for a 10-inch springform pan |
| --- |
| ½ cup softened butter |
| ¾ cup sugar |
| 4 eggs |
| 4½ oz. semi-sweet chocolate |
| 2¾ cups ground hazelnuts |
| ¾ cup plus 1 tbs. flour |
| 3 tbs. cocoa |
| 2 tsp. baking powder |
| ⅔ cup bread crumbs |
| 1 lb. red currants |
| ½ cup cassis (currant liqueur) |
| 2 tbs. superfine sugar |
| ¾ cup whipping cream |
| ½ tsp. vanilla |
| 3 tbs. powdered sugar |

**C**ream the butter with the sugar. Separate the eggs and beat the egg whites until stiff. Melt the chocolate in a bowl set in hot water and fold into the butter with the egg yolks. Add the nuts. Mix the flour with the cocoa and baking powder and fold into the batter with the egg whites. • Preheat the oven to 350°. Butter the pan and sprinkle with the bread crumbs. • Pour the batter into the pan and spread evenly. Bake 40 minutes. • Wash and pat the currants dry and remove the stems. • When the cake has cooled cut a thin slice from the top and crumble it. Sprinkle the bottom layer with the liqueur, cover with the berries and sprinkle with the sugar. Whip the cream with the vanilla and 1 tablespoon of the powdered sugar. Spread over the berries. Cover with the cake crumbs and sift powdered sugar over the top.

## Currant Cake with Meringue

### Quick and easy to make

Preparation time: 30 minutes
Baking time: 30-35 minutes

| Ingredients for 1 jelly roll |
| --- |
| 3 eggs |
| 2½ cups plus 1 tbs. sugar |
| ½ tsp. vanilla |
| 2 cups flour |
| 2 tsp. baking powder |
| ¼ scant cup butter |
| 5 tbs. milk |
| Pinch of salt |
| 2 lbs. red currants |

Separate the eggs. Beat the egg yolks with 3 tablespoons hot water until light and foamy adding 1 cup sugar a little at a time. Beat in the vanilla. Mix the flour and baking powder. Melt the butter and stir it while still warm with the milk and flour into the egg yolks and sugar. • Preheat the oven to 400°. Generously butter the jelly roll pan. • With a spatula spread the batter evenly in the pan and bake 15 minutes. • In the mean time, wash the currants, drain and remove the stems. Beat the egg whites with the salt until very stiff, adding the remaining sugar a little at a time. Fold the currants into the egg whites. • Turn the oven down to 300°. • Spread the egg white mixture onto the cake and bake in the oven 15 to 20 minutes on the middle rack of the oven. • Cut the cold cake into 20 pieces and serve freshly baked.

Tip: Instead of currants try blueberries, gooseberries or juicy pitted sweet cherries with the meringue.

# Blueberry Pie

**Specialty from England**

Preparation time: 1½ hours
Baking time: 40 minutes

Ingredients for 1 pie or a 9-inch tart pan

For the tart pastry:

2 cups flour

½ cup plus 1 tbs. butter

⅓ cup sugar

Pinch of salt

1 .egg yolk

For the filling:

2 egg whites

1 banana

2 tbs. lemon juice

1 lb. blueberries

⅔ cup sliced almonds

⅓ cup sugar

½ tsp. cinnamon

For the glaze:

1 egg yolk

2 tbs. milk

Quickly knead the flour with the butter, sugar, salt and egg yolk. Chill 1 hour. • Beat the egg whites until stiff. Peel the banana, slice thinly and sprinkle with lemon juice. Wash the blueberries. Mix the sliced almonds, sugar, cinnamon, banana and egg whites with the berries. • Preheat the oven to 400°. • Divide the tart pastry into one larger and one smaller portion. Roll out the larger part first and use it to line the pan. Brush the edges with cold water. Fill with the fruit. Roll out the smaller portion, lay on the fruit and press the edges of pastry together. Cut holes in the top. Whisk the egg yolk with the milk. Cut ornaments from the excess pastry dough. Brush the pie with egg yolk and place the pastry cut outs on top, brush again and bake 40 minutes on the lower rack of the oven until golden brown.

# Blackberry Cake

**Requires some time**

Preparation time: 1½ hours
Baking time: 1 hour

Ingredients for 1 jelly roll pan

For the yeast dough:

3 cups plus 1 tbs. flour

1 packet dry yeast

¼ scant cup butter

⅓ cup sugar

1 egg

Pinch of salt

Grated rind of ½ lemon

For the topping:

2 lbs. blackberries

5 eggs

2 cups ricotta or cottage cheese

½ cup plus 2 tbs. crème fraîche

1 cup sugar

1 package vanilla pudding mix

⅔ cup sliced almonds

2 tbs. powdered sugar

½ tsp. cinnamon

½ tsp. cinnamon

Knead the yeast dough ingredients well and set aside to rise 30 minutes. • Wash and pat the blackberries dry. • Roll out the dough on a well buttered jelly roll pan and cover with the blackberries. • Separate the eggs. Beat the egg yolks with the cheese, crème fraîche, sugar and pudding mix. Beat the egg whites until stiff and fold into the cheese mixture. Spread evenly over the berries. • Preheat the oven to 350°. • Sprinkle the sliced almonds over the cake and bake 1 hour. • Mix the powdered sugar with the cinnamon and sift over the cake.

## Raspberry Sponge Cake

### Quick and easy to make

Preparation time: 40 minutes
Baking time: 20 minutes

| Ingredients for an 11-inch springform pan |
| --- |
| 2 eggs |
| ⅓ cup plus 2 tbs. sugar |
| ½ tsp. vanilla |
| Pinch of salt |
| ⅓ cup plus 1 tbs. flour |
| ⅓ cup cornstarch |
| ½ cup cake or bread crumbs |
| 1 lb. raspberries |
| ¾ cup whipping cream |
| 3 tbs. superfine sugar |
| ¼ oz. package red gelatin |
| 1 cup water |

Separate the eggs. Beat the yolks with 2 tablespoons warm water until light and foamy, adding the sugar and va-nilla a little at a time. Beat the egg whites with the salt until stiff. Mix the flour and cornstarch and fold with the egg whites into the yolks. • Preheat the oven to 350°. Butter the pan and sprin-kle with the crumbs. Pour in the batter and bake 20 minutes on the lower rack of the oven until golden brown. Turn off the heat and leave the cake in the oven 15 minutes. Remove from pan. • Wash and drain the raspberries and drain well. Whip the cream with 1 tablespoon of the sugar. Put about ¼ of the cream in a pastry bag and chill. • Spread the rest of the cream on the cooled cake and cover with the berries. • Prepare a glaze from the gelatin, the remaining sugar and the water. Allow to cool somewhat and pour onto the berries starting in the middle and moving out. Allow 30 minutes to gel, garnish the cake with the chilled cream and serve immedi-ately.

## Strawberry Butter Cake

### Easy to make

Preparation time: 15 minutes
Baking time: 20 minutes
Time to put the cake together: 30 minutes

| Ingredients for an 11-inch springform pan |
| --- |
| ⅓ cup butter |
| ⅓ cup plus 2 tbs. sugar |
| ½ tsp. vanilla |
| 2 eggs |
| 1¼ cups flour |
| 1 tsp. baking powder |
| Pinch of salt |
| 4 tbs. milk |
| 1 tsp. gelatin |
| ½ cup ricotta or cottage cheese |
| 5 tbs. superfine sugar |
| ¾ cup whipping cream |
| 1 lb. strawberries |

Cream the butter with the sugar, vanilla and eggs. Mix the flour with the baking powder and salt and add to the butter and eggs alternately with the milk a little at a time. • Preheat the oven to 400°. • Pour the bat-ter into the greased pan. Bake the cake 20 minutes on the lower rack of the oven until golden brown and turn out im-mediately. • Dissolve the gelatin in a tablespoon of cold water. Beat the cheese with 3 table-spoons of the sugar and add the dissolved gelatin. • Whip the cream with the remaining sugar and fold one half into the cheese. • Wash and dry the strawberries. Cut off the stems and halve the larger berries. • Spread the cheese mixture on the cake, cover with the berries and decorate with small mounds of whipped cream.

## Strawberry Cheese Cake

**Requires some time**

Preparation time: 1 hour
Baking time: 1¼ hours
Time to put the cake together:
20 minutes

| |
|---|
| Ingredients for an 11-inch springform pan |
| For the tart pastry: |
| 1½ cups plus 1 tbs. flour |
| Generous pinch baking powder |
| ⅔ cup sugar |
| ½ tsp. vanilla |
| 1 egg yolk |
| ½ scant cup butter |
| For the topping: |
| 2 cups ricotta or cottage cheese |
| 3 eggs |
| 1 egg white |
| ½ scant cup butter |
| 1 cup sugar |
| ½ lemon |
| ½ cup plus 2 tbs. crème fraîche |
| ⅓ cup cornstarch |
| 1 lb. strawberries |
| ¼ oz. package red gelatin |
| ½ cup whipping cream |
| ½ tsp. vanilla |
| 1 tbs. powdered sugar |

Quickly knead the tart pastry ingredients into a smooth dough and chill. • Drain the cheese and separate the eggs. Cream the butter with the sugar and add the egg yolks. Mix the rind from the ½ lemon into the butter and sugar. Add the juice. Beat with the crème fraîche and the cheese. Beat the egg whites until stiff and fold into the cheese mixture with the cornstarch. • Preheat the oven to 350°. Roll out the pastry dough and use it to line the lightly greased pan. Bake 15 minutes. • Pour in the cheese mixture and bake 1 hour on the bottom rack of the oven. • Wash and halve the strawberries. • Prepare the gelatin. • Spread the strawberries on the cheese cake and cover with the gelatin. Let the glaze gel. • Beat the cream with the vanilla and

sugar until stiff, put into a pastry bag and pipe decorations on the cake.

## One-Layer Gooseberry Cake

### Requires some time

Preparation time: 1½ hours
Baking time: 45 minutes

| Ingredients for 1 jelly roll pan |
| --- |
| 2 cups flour |
| 2 tbs. sugar |
| Pinch of salt |
| Grated rind of 1 lemon |
| 1 tsp. dry yeast |
| ½ cup lukewarm milk |
| 1 egg |
| For the topping: |
| 2 slices zwieback |
| 2 lbs. gooseberries |
| For the custard: |
| ⅔ cup butter |
| ⅔ cup sugar |
| 4 eggs |
| ⅓ cup plus 1 tbs. flour |
| Pinch of salt |
| ½ cup whipping cream |

Sift the flour into a bowl and make a well in the center. Scatter the sugar, salt and lemon rind around the edges. Stir the yeast in the center with a little of the milk and some of the flour. Set aside 30 minutes for the sponge to form. • Crush the zwieback in a plastic bag with a rolling pin. Wash the gooseberries and drain well. • For the custard beat the butter with the sugar and the eggs. Stir in the flour, salt and cream. • Knead the yeast sponge with the rest of the flour, milk and the egg and set aside 15 minutes to rise. • Generously butter a jelly roll pan. Roll the dough out in it and allow to rise 15 minutes longer. •

Preheat the oven to 400°. • Scatter first the zwieback crumbs and then the berries over the dough. Pour the custard over the berries. • Bake the cake 45 minutes on the bottom rack of the oven.

## Apricot-Gooseberry Cake

### Quick and easy to make

Preparation time: 30 minutes
Baking time: 45 minutes

| Ingredients for an 11-inch springform pan |
| --- |
| ¾ cup ricotta or cottage cheese |
| ¾ cup sugar |
| Grated rind of 1 lemon |
| Pinch of salt |
| 6 tbs. vegetable oil |
| 4 tbs. milk |
| 2⅓ cups flour |
| 1 tbs. baking powder |
| ⅔ cup bread crumbs |
| 1 lb. fully ripe apricots |
| ½ lb. gooseberries |

Drain the cheese and beat with the sugar, lemon rind, salt, oil and milk. Combine the flour and baking powder and stir into the cheese mixture 1 tablespoon at a time. Briefly knead the dough. • Preheat the oven to 400°. Generously butter the pan and sprinkle with bread crumbs. • On a floured surface roll out the dough, line the pan with it, shaping 1-inch sides. • Wash, dry, halve and pit the apricots. Place them, round side up, on the dough. Wash and dry the gooseberries, spread them between the apricots and press them gently into the dough. • Bake the cake 45 minutes.

## Apricot Cheese Cake Slices

**Requires some time**

Preparation time: 1¼ hours
Baking time: 1 hour

| Ingredients for 1 jelly roll pan |
| --- |
| 3¾ cups plus 1 tbs. flour |
| 1½ tsp. dry yeast |
| 1 cup lukewarm milk |
| ⅓ cup plus 2 tbs. sugar |
| 2 eggs |
| ⅓ cup melted butter |
| For the topping: |
| 1½ lbs. fully ripe apricots |
| 3 cups ricotta or cottage cheese |
| 7 tbs. butter |
| 1 cup sugar |
| 3 eggs |
| Grated rind of 1 lemon |
| 1 tbs. lemon juice |
| 1 package vanilla pudding mix |
| 1 tbs. cornstarch |

| For the streusel: |
| --- |
| 1 cup flour |
| ⅓ cup sugar |
| ¼ cup butter |
| ½ tsp. vanilla |

**K**nead the flour with the yeast, milk, sugar, eggs and butter. Set aside to rise 30 minutes. • Wash and pat the apricots dry, halve and pit them. Drain the cheese. • Roll out the dough and use it to line a greased jelly roll pan. Set aside to rise 20 minutes. • Cream the butter with the sugar. Separate the eggs and mix the yolks with the butter and sugar. Beat the egg whites until stiff. Beat the lemon rind and juice, the pudding mix and the cornstarch with the cheese and combine with the butter mixture. Fold in the egg whites. • Preheat the oven to 400°. • Spread the cheese mixture on the dough and press the apricot halves gen-tly into the cheese. • Bake the cake 40 minutes. • Put the streusel together from the remaining ingredients, sprinkle it over the cake and bake 20 minutes longer.

## Apricot-Almond Cream Cake

**Requires some time**

Preparation time: 1 hour
Baking time: 45 minutes

| Ingredients for 1 jelly roll pan |
| --- |
| 3¾ cups plus 1 tbs. flour |
| 1 tsp. baking powder |
| 1 cup sugar |
| ½ tsp. vanilla |
| Pinch of salt |
| 2 egg yolks |
| 1 egg |
| 1 cup plus 2 tbs. butter |
| 3 lbs. apricots |
| 1 cup whipping cream |
| ⅔ cups superfine sugar |
| 1⅓ cups blanched almonds |

**Q**uickly knead the flour with the baking powder, sugar, vanilla, salt, 1 egg yolk, egg and flaked butter. Chill 30 minutes. • Wash, dry, halve and pit the apricots. • Whip the cream very stiff, adding the sugar very gradually while whipping. Grind half the almonds and fold into the cream with the remaining yolk. • Preheat the oven to 400°. • Roll out the dough, lay it out in the pan and prick well with a fork. Press the apricot halves, curved side down, gently into the dough. Place 1 almond in each apricot. • Pour the almond cream over the fruit and bake 45 minutes on the bottom rack of the oven.

## Apricot Cake with Marzipan

**Easy to make**

Preparation time: 45 minutes
Baking time: 40 minutes

| Ingredients for 1 jelly roll pan |
| --- |
| ½ cup ricotta or cottage cheese |
| 1¼ cups milk |
| 5 tbs. vegetable oil |
| ⅓ cup plus 2 tbs. sugar |
| 2 cups flour |
| 3 tsp. baking powder |
| ½ package vanilla pudding mix |
| 1 tsp. cornstarch |
| 2 oz. almond paste |
| 1½ lbs. apricots |
| ½ cup apricot marmalade |
| ¾ cup sliced almonds |

**B**eat the well-drained cheese with ¼ cup milk, oil and all but 1 tablespoon of the sugar. Mix the flour with the baking powder, stir half into the cheese mixture and knead in the rest. • Beat 4 tablespoons of the milk with the pudding mix, the remaining sugar and the cornstarch. Bring the remaining milk to a boil, pour in the pudding mixture, bring to a boil again and remove from the heat. Dissolve the almond paste in the hot liquid. • Preheat the oven to 400°. Grease a jelly roll pan with oil. • Roll the dough out in the pan and spread with the cooled pudding. • Pit the apricots and spread out on the cake. Bake 45 minutes on the bottom rack of the oven. • Brush the cake with the heated marmalade and scatter the almond slices over it.

## Cherry Pie with Almonds

**Inexpensive, somewhat difficult**

Preparation time: 1½ hours
Baking time: 45 minutes

| Ingredients for a 9-inch tart pan |
| --- |
| 2⅓ cups flour |
| 1 tsp. baking powder |
| ⅔ cup butter |
| 1 cup sugar |
| ½ tsp. vanilla |
| 1½ lbs. sweet cherries |
| 2 tbs. cornstarch |
| 1½ cups cherry juice |
| 2 tbs. cherry liqueur |
| 1¼ cups chopped almonds |
| 1 egg yolk |

**Q**uickly knead a smooth pastry dough from the flour, baking powder, butter, ⅔ cup of the sugar and vanilla. Chill 1 hour. • Wash, dry and pit the cherries. Beat the cornstarch with the remaining sugar and 5 tablespoons of the juice. Bring the remaining juice to a boil, remove from the heat and stir in the cornstarch mixture and the cherries. Boil 1 minute stirring constantly. Allow to cool. • Preheat the oven to 400°. • Roll out the dough and use it to line the buttered pan. Prick the bottom well with a fork and bake 20 minutes. • Stir the liqueur into the cherries. Pour into the pie crust and sprinkle with almonds. Roll out the remaining dough and cut ¾-inch strips with a pie jagger to make a lattice of pastry on the pie. Brush with the beaten egg yolk. • Allow the pie to stand 4 hours before cutting.

## Cherry-Nut Torte

**Easy to make**

Preparation time: 25 minutes
Baking time: 1 hour

Ingredients for an 11-inch
springform pan

1 lb. sour cherries

⅔ cup softened butter

1 cup sugar

4 eggs

4 oz. bittersweet chocolate

1½ cups ground hazelnuts

⅔ cup cake or bread crumbs

1 tbs. powdered sugar

**W**ash, dry and pit the cherries. • Cream the butter with the sugar. Separate the eggs. Grate the chocolate. Beat the egg whites until stiff. Stir the yolks one after another into the butter and sugar. Add the chocolate and the ground nuts and fold in the egg whites. • Preheat the oven to 350°. Butter the pan and sprinkle with the crumbs. • Pour the batter into the pan and cover with cherries. Bake 1 hour on the bottom rack of the oven. • Turn off the heat and leave the cherry cake in the oven 10 minutes to cool. • When cool sift the powdered sugar over the cake.

## Cherry Sponge Cake with Kiwis

**Easy to make**

Preparation time: 20 minutes
Baking time: 20 minutes
Time to put the cake together:
35 minutes

Ingredients for an 11-inch
springform pan

1 lb. cherries

1 tbs. lemon juice

2 eggs

⅓ cup plus 2 tbs. sugar

½ tsp. vanilla

⅓ cup plus 1 tbs. cake flour

⅓ cup cornstarch

2 packages unflavored gelatin
(¼ oz. each)

½ cup plus 2 tbs. crème fraîche

2 tbs. milk

⅓ cup sugar

3-4 kiwis

2 tbs. sugar

1 cup apple juice

**P**it and cook the cherries with the lemon juice in 1 cup water for 5 minutes. • Separate the eggs. Beat the yolks with 2 tablespoons warm water, the sugar and vanilla. Beat the egg whites until stiff and fold into the egg yolk mixture with the flour and cornstarch. • Preheat the oven to 350°. Pour the batter into the pan and bake 20 minutes. Turn the heat off and leave the cake in the oven 10 minutes. • Dissolve 1 package gelatin in 1 tablespoon cold water. Mix the crème fraîche with the milk and sugar. Stir in the dissolved gelatin. Spread the cream mixture on the sponge cake. Arrange the cherries around the outside edge. Peel and slice the kiwis and use to decorate the cake. • For the glaze, bring the remaining package of gelatin to a boil with the sugar and apple juice. Pour it over the cake.

## Cherry Cheese Cake

**Inexpensive and easy to make**

Preparation time: 45 minutes
Baking time: 1 hour

Ingredients for an 11-inch springform pan

For the butter cake batter:

| | |
|---|---|
| 7 tbs. butter | |
| ¾ cup sugar | |
| ½ tsp. vanilla | |
| 2 eggs | |
| 1¼ cups flour | |
| ⅓ cup plus 1 tbs. cornstarch | |
| 1 tsp. baking powder | |

For the topping:

| | |
|---|---|
| 1 lb. sweet cherries | |
| 4 eggs | |
| ⅔ cup butter | |
| 1 cup sugar | |
| 1 tsp. vanilla | |
| 3 cups ricotta or cottage cheese | |
| ¾ cup cornstarch | |

Preheat the oven to 350° and butter the pan. • Cream the butter with the sugar and vanilla, add the eggs. Mix the flour, cornstarch, and baking powder together and add to the first mixture. • Pour the batter into the pan and bake 20 minutes. • Wash, dry and pit the cherries. Separate the eggs. • Beat the butter with the sugar, vanilla and egg yolks. Beat the egg whites until stiff. Combine the cheese with the first mixture and fold in the egg whites, cornstarch and cherries. • Spread the cheese mixture on the cake and bake 50 minutes longer. Turn off the heat and leave in the oven 10 minutes.

## Cherry Streusel Cake

**Easy to make**

Preparation time: 30 minutes
Baking time: 40 minutes

Ingredients for a 10-inch springform pan

| | |
|---|---|
| 1⅓ cups butter | |
| 1 lb. sour cherries | |
| 1⅓ cups sugar | |
| 3¾ cups plus 1 tbs. flour | |
| 1 tbs. baking powder | |
| ½ tsp. grated lemon rind | |
| Pinch of salt | |
| 1 tsp. cinnamon | |
| 1 egg | |
| ⅓ cup blanched almonds | |

Melt the butter over low heat and allow to cool somewhat. • Wash, dry and pit the cherries and sprinkle with 2 tablespoons of the sugar. • In a mixing bowl combine the flour, baking powder, remaining sugar, the lemon rind, salt, cinnamon and egg. Add the melted butter and use the dough hook on the electric mixer to work it into a crumbly dough. • Preheat the oven to 400°. Generously butter the pan. • Press half the dough into the pan and scatter the almonds over it. Cover with the cherries and top with the remaining dough. • Bake 40 minutes on the middle rack until golden brown. • Open the springform pan and allow the cake to cool. • This cake is good fresh but tastes fine after one or two days.

## Cherry Cake with Chocolate

**Nutritious, quick to make**

Preparation time: 30 minutes
Baking time: 45 minutes

Ingredients for a 9-inch springform pan

1¼ cups whole-wheat flour

⅓ cup plus 1 tbs. whole-grain rye flour

3 tbs. cocoa

1 tsp. baking powder

½ tsp. cinnamon

½ tsp. ground coriander

1⅓ cups blanched almonds

¾ cup plus 2 tbs. butter

¾ cup honey

4 eggs

2 tbs. rum

1 lb. sour cherries

Scant ½ lb. honey-sweetened chocolate

⅔ cups sliced almonds

**M**ix all the flour with the cocoa, baking powder, cinnamon and coriander. Grind the almonds and add to the flour mixture. • Cream the butter with the honey and gradually stir in the dry ingredients, eggs and rum. • Preheat the oven to 350°. Butter the pan. • Spread the batter evenly in the pan. • Wash and drain the cherries and remove the stems and pits. Spread them out on the batter and gently press them in. • Bake the cake 45 minutes on the middle rack. Turn off the heat and leave in the oven 10 minutes longer. • Melt the chocolate in a bowl set in hot water. Spread on the cake and sprinkle with sliced almonds.

## Cherry-Oatmeal Cake

**Quick and easy to make**

Preparation time: 15 minutes
Baking time: 35-40 minutes

Ingredients for 1 jelly roll pan

2 lbs. sweet cherries

1⅓ cups softened butter

1¼ cups plus 1 tbs. sugar

½ tsp. vanilla

4 eggs

Grated rind of 1 lemon

2¼ cups finely shredded rolled oats

1½ cups plus 1 tbs. whole-wheat flour

1 tsp. baking powder

2 tbs. rum

2 tbs. coarse oat flakes

⅓ cup sugar

⅔ cup grated coconut

**P**reheat the oven to 400°. Butter the pan. • Wash, dry and pit the cherries. • Cream the butter with the sugar and vanilla. Add the eggs one at a time, then add the lemon rind. Mix the rolled oats with the flour and baking powder and stir into the first mixture with the rum, a tablespoon at a time. • Spread the dough evenly in the pan and cover with cherries. Mix the oat flakes with the coconut and sugar and sprinkle over the cherries. • Bake 35 to 40 minutes on the middle rack of the oven until pale yellow. • With a knife dipped in cold water cut the cake into 20 pieces while still warm. Cool on a cake rack. • Vanilla-flavored whipped cream goes very well with this cake.

## Peach Pastry

### Easy to make

Preparation time: 50 minutes
Baking time: 1 hour

| Ingredients for a 9-inch tart pan |
| --- |
| 3 eggs |
| 2 cups flour |
| Generous pinch baking powder |
| ⅔ cup butter |
| ¾ cup sugar |
| 1¼ cups ground almonds |
| 1 tbs. lemon juice |
| 3 tbs. rum |
| 1 lb. fully ripe peaches |
| ⅔ chopped almonds |
| 3 tbs. apricot jam |

Separate the eggs. • With cold hands quickly knead a smooth dough from the flour, baking powder, butter, ⅓ cup of the sugar and 1 egg yolk. Chill 30 minutes. • Beat the egg whites until stiff. Beat the ground almonds with the remaining egg yolks and sugar, the lemon juice and 2 tablespoons of the rum. Fold in the egg whites. • Preheat the oven to 350° and butter the pan. Bake the crust 25 minutes. • Skin, halve and pit the peaches. • Fill the baked crust with the almond mixture and bake 15 minutes. Press the peaches into the almond filling and bake 20 minutes longer. • Toast the chopped almonds in a dry pan until golden brown. • Stir the jam with the remaining rum and heat, stirring constantly. Brush on the warm cake. Sprinkle with the almonds.

## Peach Cheese Cake

### Requires some time

Preparation time: 1 hour
Baking time: 1 hour

| Ingredients for a 10-inch springform pan |
| --- |
| 2 cups ricotta or cottage cheese |
| 3 tbs. milk |
| 3 tbs. vegetable oil |
| ¾ cup sugar |
| 1½ cups plus 1 tbs. flour |
| 2 tsp. baking powder |
| ½ cup whipping cream |
| 1 tsp. vanilla |
| 3 eggs |
| 1 tbs. cornstarch |
| 2 tbs. farina |
| 1 lb. peaches |
| 2 tbs. powdered sugar |

Drain the cheese. Beat ¼ cup plus 1 tablespoon of the cheese with the milk, oil and 2 tablespoons of the sugar. Mix the flour with the baking powder and stir, then knead into the first mixture. • Grease the pan well. Roll out the dough and use it to line the pan, shaping 1-inch sides. • Mix the cream with the remaining sugar and vanilla. Separate the eggs and stir the egg yolks into the cream. Beat the egg whites until stiff. Mix the cornstarch with the farina and mix with the remaining cheese into the egg-cream mixture. Fold in the egg whites. • Preheat the oven to 400°. • Briefly dip the peaches in boiling water. Skin, halve and pit them. • Spoon ⅓ of the cheese mixture into the springform pan. Cover with the peach halves and top with the remaining cheese mixture. • Bake the cake 1 hour on the bottom rack. Turn off the heat and leave in the oven 10 minutes longer. • Sift powdered sugar over the cooled cake.

# Peach Cake with Almonds

**Requires some time**

Preparation time: 1 hour
Baking time: 40 minutes

| Ingredients for a 10-inch springform pan |
| --- |
| 2 cups flour |
| ⅔ cup cornstarch |
| ⅔ cup ground almonds |
| 3 eggs |
| ¾ cup plus 1 tbs. softened butter |
| Pinch of salt |
| 1½ cups sugar |
| 1 tsp. vanilla |
| 2 lbs. peaches |
| ⅔ cup sliced almonds |
| ¾ cup plus 1 tbs. crème fraîche |
| Grated rind of ½ lemon |

**P**lace the flour with ⅓ cup of the cornstarch and the almonds in a bowl. Add 1 egg, the butter, salt, ⅔ cup of the sugar and ½ teaspoon vanilla. • Briefly dip the peaches in boiling water, then skin, halve and pit them. Bring 1 cup of water to a boil with ⅓ cup of sugar. Simmer the peach halves 15 minutes and drain well. • Preheat the oven to 350°. Grease the pan. • Spread the dough on the bottom of the pan and press into sides about 1-inch high. Bake the crust 15 minutes. • Lay the peach halves in the crust and sprinkle with the sliced almonds. Separate the remaining eggs. Beat the yolks with the remaining sugar and vanilla and add the crème fraîche, lemon rind and remaining cornstarch. Beat the egg whites until stiff and fold into the sponge cake batter. Distribute the batter evenly over the peaches and bake 25 minutes longer. • Allow the peach cake to cool somewhat, then open the springform pan, remove the cake and cool on a cake rack.

## Plum Tart

### Easy to make, a famous recipe

Preparation time: 50 minutes
Baking time: 35 minutes

| Ingredients for an 11-inch springform pan |
| --- |
| 2 cups flour |
| ⅓ cup sugar |
| Generous pinch of salt |
| 7 tbs. butter |
| ½ cup cold water |
| 2 tsp. vinegar |
| 2 lbs. small plums |
| ½ cup whipping cream |
| 2 eggs |
| Generous pinch cinnamon |

Using the dough hook on the mixer knead the flour with 1 tablespoon of the sugar, the salt, flaked butter, water and vinegar. Then knead with very cold hands to form a smooth rich tart pastry. • Wash, dry, halve and pit the plums. • Butter the pan and preheat the oven to 400°. • On a work surface dusted with flour, roll out the dough into a circle. Set in the bottom of the pan and shape sides ¾-inch high. Set the plums, round side down, evenly in a rosette shape to cover the dough. • Bake 10 minutes on the middle rack of the oven. • Beat the cream with the eggs, the remaining sugar and the cinnamon, pour over the plums and bake 25 minutes longer. If desired, sprinkle powdered sugar over the cooled tart shortly before serving.

# Plum Datschi Sheet Tart

**A famous recipe**

Preparation time: 45 minutes
Rising time: 45 minutes
Baking time: 30 minutes

Ingredients for 1 jelly roll pan

1½ tsp. dry yeast

1 tbs. sugar

¾ cup lukewarm milk

3 cups plus 1 tbs. flour

Pinch of salt

1 egg

⅔ cup sugar

⅓ cup melted butter

2½ lbs. plums

⅔ cups chopped almonds

½ tsp. cinnamon

**M**ix the yeast and sugar with the milk, cover and let stand 15 minutes. • Mix half the flour, the salt, egg, ⅓ cup plus 2 tablespoons of the sugar and the melted butter with the yeast sponge. Knead in the rest of the flour a little at a time. The dough should come away from the sides of the pan. If it is still sticky, add a little more flour. Cover and set aside to rise 30 minutes. • Wash, dry, and pit the plums. Cut into quarters. • Knead the dough thoroughly. Generously butter the jelly roll pan and roll the dough out on it. • Lay the plums on the dough. • Preheat the oven to 425°. • Bake the Datschi 30 minutes on the bottom rack of the oven. • Mix the remaining sugar with the cinnamon and sprinkle evenly over the tart. • Serve with sweetened whipped cream.

# Plum Upside-Down Cake

**Quick and easy to make**

Preparation time: 30 minutes
Baking time: 1 hour

Ingredients for a 10-inch springform pan

1 lb. plums

7 tbs. softened butter

1 cup sugar

½ tsp. vanilla

3 eggs

¾ cup plus 1 tbs. cake flour

¾ cup cornstarch

3 tsp. baking powder

⅔ cup chopped almonds

3 tbs. sugar crystals

**W**ash, dry, halve and pit the plums. • Preheat the oven to 350°. Turn the springform pan upside down and lay a piece of aluminum foil over the bottom, pressing the edges down along the sides of the pan. Turn the pan right side up and set the foil in the bottom. Butter generously. • Cream the butter with the sugar and vanilla. Add the eggs one at a time. Mix the flour with the cornstarch and baking powder and fold into the first mixture, 1 tablespoon at a time. • Lay the plums with the cut side up in the pan and pour in the batter. Spread evenly and bake 1 hour on the middle rack of the oven. • Open the springform pan and allow the cake to cool 10 minutes, then turn out onto a platter. Remove the aluminum foil. • Toast the almonds in a dry pan until golden brown. When cool sprinkle over the cake with the sugar.

## Grape Whole-Wheat Cake

**Nutritious**

Preparation time: 1¼ hours
Baking time: 50 minutes

Ingredients for a 10-inch springform pan

⅓ cup softened butter

3 tbs. honey

2 egg yolks

1½ cups plus 1 tbs. whole-wheat flour

1⅓ cups hazelnuts

2 tbs. sesame seeds

1 lb. white grapes

4 eggs

1 cup Italian cream cheese or crème fraîche

7 tbs. sugar beet syrup or golden syrup

Juice and grated rind of 1 lemon

Cream the butter with the honey and egg yolks. Mix the flour with the nuts and sesame seeds and stir into the first mixture 1 tablespoon at a time. Knead the dough, which should be smooth and firm. Chill 1 hour. • Wash and drain the grapes and remove the stems. • Separate the eggs and beat the yolks with the cream cheese or crème fraîche, syrup, lemon juice and lemon rind. Beat the egg whites until stiff and fold in. • Preheat the oven to 350° and lightly butter the pan. • Roll out the pastry dough and use it to line the pan, shaping 1-inch sides. Fill with the custard and sprinkle in the grapes. Bake 50 minutes.

## Grape Cake

**Requires some time**

Preparation time: 1½ hours
Baking time: 1 hours

Ingredients for a 10-inch springform pan

For the tart pastry:

1¾ cups flour

½ cup butter

1 egg yolk

⅓ cup plus 2 tbs. sugar

Grated rind of ½ lemon

1 tbs. rum

For the filling:

1 lb. white grapes

5 egg yolks

⅓ cup sugar

1 vanilla bean

1¾ cups plus 2 tbs. ground almonds

6 egg whites

⅓ cup plus 1 tbs. flour

Quickly knead the ingredients for the tart pastry and chill covered 1 hour. • Wash the grapes, remove the stems and seeds. • Beat the egg yolks with the sugar until lemon colored. Slit the vanilla bean and scrape out the soft seed mass. Add with the almonds to the egg-sugar mixture. Beat the egg whites until stiff and fold in with the flour. • Preheat the oven to 350°. • On a floured surface roll out the pastry dough, use it to line the pan and shape 1-inch sides. • Stir the grapes with the sponge cake and pour into the pan. Bake 1 hour on the middle rack of the oven. • If desired, spread the cake with sugar icing and garnish with grapes.

# Banana Cake with Vanilla Pudding

## Quick and inexpensive

Preparation time: 45 minutes
Baking time: 20 minutes

Ingredients for an 11-inch springform pan

For the batter:

3 eggs

⅔ cup sugar

½ tsp. vanilla

½ cup plus 1 tbs. sifted cake flour

½ cup cornstarch

Pinch of salt

½ cup cake or bread crumbs

For the topping:

½ package vanilla pudding mix

1 tbs. sugar

1 cup milk

3 large firm bananas

1 tbs. lemon juice

For the glaze:

¼ oz. package gelatin

1 tbs. sugar

½ cup water

Separate the eggs and beat the egg yolks until light and foamy with 2 tablespoons warm water. Gradually add the sugar and vanilla. Mix the flour with the cornstarch. Beat the egg whites and salt until stiff, add with the flour to the first mixture and fold in. • Preheat the oven to 350°. Butter the bottom of the pan and sprinkle with sponge cake or bread crumbs. Pour in the batter and bake 20 minutes on the lower rack of the oven. Turn the heat off and leave the cake in the oven 15 minutes longer. Let it cool in the pan, then turn out. • Beat the pudding mix with the sugar and 3 tablespoons of the milk. Bring the rest of the milk to a boil, add the pudding, boil again and cool.

Spread on the cake. Peel and slice the bananas and arrange on the pudding. Sprinkle with the lemon juice. • Make a glaze from the remaining ingredients and spread it evenly over the bananas.

# Banana Butter Cake

## Inexpensive and easy to make

Preparation time: 30 minutes
Baking time: 1¼ hours

Ingredients for 1 tube pan

7 tbs. butter

4 medium very ripe bananas

½ cup whipping cream

3 eggs

1½ cups sugar

1 vanilla bean

3 cups plus 1 tbs. flour

1 tbs. baking powder

⅔ cup bread crumbs

4 oz. bittersweet chocolate

Melt the butter. Peel the bananas, mash with a fork and mix with the cream. Beat the eggs with the sugar until lemon colored. Slit the vanilla bean, scrape out the soft center and add. Mix the flour with the baking powder and stir into the egg-sugar mixture with the melted butter. Stir in the mashed bananas. • Preheat the oven to 350°. • Generously butter a tube pan and sprinkle with bread crumbs. Pour in the batter and spread evenly. Bake 1 hour and 15 minutes. • Melt the chocolate in a bowl set in hot water and pour over the banana cake. Sprinkle with chopped pistachios if desired.

## Pineapple-Marzipan Cake

**Easy to make, somewhat expensive**

Preparation time: 30 minutes
Baking time: 50 minutes

Ingredients for an 11-inch loaf pan

| | |
|---|---|
| ⅔ cup bread crumbs | |
| 8 oz. almond paste | |
| ⅔ cup softened butter | |
| 1 cup sugar | |
| ½ tsp. vanilla | |
| 3 eggs | |
| 2⅓ cups flour | |
| ⅓ cup cornstarch | |
| 2 tsp. baking powder | |
| 2 slices pineapple | |
| 1 tbs. coconut oil | |
| 2 oz. bittersweet chocolate | |
| 1 slice candied pineapple | |

**P**reheat the oven to 400°. Butter the pan and sprinkle with the crumbs. • Cut the almond paste into pieces and beat with the butter, sugar and vanilla. Add the eggs one at a time. Mix the flour with the cornstarch and baking powder and stir into the first mixture 1 tablespoon at a time. Chop the pineapple and stir in. • Pour the batter into the pan and bake 50 minutes on the middle rack. Turn off the heat and leave the cake in the oven 10 minutes longer. • Remove the cake from the pan and cool on a cake rack. • Melt the coconut oil. Cut the chocolate into small pieces and melt in the oil. Glaze the cake with the chocolate. Cut the candied pineapple into pieces and use them to garnish the cake.

## Sunken Pineapple Cake

**Nutritious, quick to make**

Preparation time: 40 minutes
Baking time: 40 minutes

Ingredients for an 11-inch springform pan

| | |
|---|---|
| 1¼ cups whole-wheat flour | |
| ⅓ cup plus 1 tbs. millet flour | |
| ⅓ cup plus 1 tbs. buckwheat flour | |
| 3 tbs. cornstarch | |
| 1 tsp. ground anise | |
| 2 tsp. baking powder | |
| 2 oz. light sesame seeds | |
| 2 oz. bittersweet chocolate | |
| ⅔ cup softened butter | |
| ⅔ cup liquid honey | |
| 4 eggs | |
| 1 pineapple (about 2 lbs.) | |
| 3 tbs. maple syrup | |
| Juice of 1 lime | |

**M**ix all the flour with the cornstarch, anise, baking powder and half the sesame seeds. Coarsely grate the chocolate and add to the dry ingredients. Cream the butter with the honey. Stir in the eggs and the dry ingredients alternately. • Preheat the oven to 350°. • Quarter and peel the pineapple and remove the hard core. Cut the fruit into pieces and spread on the batter, pressing in gently. • Bake 40 minutes on the middle rack, then turn the heat off and leave the cake in the oven 10 minutes longer. • Whisk the maple syrup with the lime juice and spread on the cake. • Cool the cake in the pan.

## Pineapple Custard Pie

### Quick and easy to make

Preparation time: 30 minutes
Baking time: 40 minutes

| Ingredients for a 9-inch tart pan |
| --- |
| 4 oz. (½ cup) ricotta or cottage cheese |
| 2 tbs. milk |
| 3 tbs. vegetable oil |
| ¾ cup sugar |
| Pinch of salt |
| 1½ cups plus 1 tbs. flour |
| 2 tsp. baking powder |
| 1 pineapple (about 2 lbs.) |
| 2 eggs |
| ½ tsp. grated lemon rind |
| 1 cup sour cream |

Preheat the oven to 400°. Butter the pan. • Knead the drained cheese with the milk, oil, ⅓ cup of the sugar, the salt, 1¼ cups of the flour and the baking powder first with the dough hook on the electric mixer and then by hand. Form a smooth dough. • On a floured surface roll out two-thirds of the dough to line the bottom of the pan. From the rest make a long roll and from it shape the sides. • Quarter and peel the pineapple and remove the tough core. Cut the fruit into pieces. • Separate the eggs. Beat the yolks with the remaining sugar and lemon rind until lemon colored. Add the remaining flour and the sour cream alternately. Beat the egg whites until stiff and fold into the batter. • Spread the pieces of pineapple on the pastry and pour in the custard. • Bake 40 minutes on the middle rack of the oven. • Allow the pie to cool 5 minutes, then remove from the pan and cool on a cake rack.

## Apple-Rhubarb Slices with Vanilla Cream

### Requires some time

Preparation time: 1½ hours
Baking time: 35 minutes
Time to put the cake together: 1 hour

Ingredients for 1 jelly roll pan

For the dough:

3 cups plus 1 tbs. flour

1 tsp. baking powder

1 egg

¾ cup sugar

Pinch of salt

1 cup plus 2 tbs. butter

For the topping:

4 lbs. rhubarb

2 lbs. apples

1½ cups sugar

½ tsp. cinnamon

½ tsp. ground coriander

½ cup water

1 tbs. bread crumbs

For the glaze:

2 packages red gelatin

4 tbs. sugar

For the vanilla cream:

2 tsp. gelatin

2 cups milk

1½ packages vanilla pudding mix

3 tbs. sugar

1 cup whipping cream

Using the dough hook on an electric mixer mix the flour with the baking powder, egg, sugar, salt and flaked butter. Then knead quickly by hand. Shape the dough into a ball, wrap it in aluminum foil and chill 1 hour. • Cut the ends from the stalks of rhubarb, remove the strings, wash and cut the stalks into 1-inch pieces. Quarter, peel, core and slice the apples. • Mix the fruit in a saucepan with the sugar, cinnamon and coriander. Add the water, cover and simmer 5 minutes. Drain the fruit in a sieve, retaining the juice. • Butter a jelly roll pan. Preheat the oven to 425°. On a floured surface roll out the dough to the size of the jelly roll pan, dust with flour, roll up and lay out on the pan. Prick well with a fork. Bake 5 minutes on the middle rack of the oven, then sprinkle with the bread crumbs. Spread the fruit on the pastry dough. • Bake another 30 minutes and allow to cool. Add enough water to the rhubarb and apple juice to make 2 cups and prepare the gelatin glaze according to the package directions with the sugar and juice. • Spread the glaze evenly over the cake and allow to stiffen. • For the vanilla cream dissolve the gelatin in a little water. Whisk 6 tablespoons of the milk with the pudding mix and sugar. Bring the rest of the milk to a boil. Mix in the pudding, bring to a boil and cool the mixture, stirring constantly. Whip the cream until stiff. Mix 2 tablespoons of the whipped cream with the dissolved gelatin and stir this mixture back into the whipped cream. • Using a wire whisk fold the whipped cream into the vanilla pudding. Put the vanilla cream in a pastry bag fitted with a large flower tip and pipe a lattice design on the cake. Cut the cake into 24 pieces.

## Alsatian Apple Tarts

**Easy to make, inexpensive**

Preparation time: 1½ hours
Baking time: 25 minutes

Ingredients for 12 tartlet pans

For the tart pastry:

2 cups flour

½ cup plus 1 tbs. butter

⅔ cup powdered sugar

Pinch of salt

Grated rind of 1 lemon

1 cup ground hazelnuts

1 egg yolk

For the filling:

1 lb. small tart apples

⅔ cup crème fraîche

2 eggs

⅓ cup sugar

½ tsp. vanilla

2 tbs. lemon juice

2 tbs. powdered sugar

With cold hands knead the ingredients for the tart pastry, shape the dough into a ball, cover and chill 1 hour. • Peel, quarter, core and slice the apples. • Whisk the crème fraîche with the eggs, sugar, vanilla and lemon juice. • Preheat the oven to 425°. Lightly butter the tart pans. • Roll out the pastry dough to a thin sheet and use it to line the tart pans. Fill with the apples and bake 5 minutes. Turn the heat down to 350°. Pour in the custard and bake 20 minutes longer. • Sift powdered sugar over the tartlets.

## Rhubarb Tartlets

**Requires some time**

Preparation time: 1¼ hours
Baking time: 20 minutes

Ingredients for 8 tart pans

1 cup flour

1 cup sugar

½ tsp. vanilla

2 pinches salt

1 egg yolk

3½ tbs. cold butter

½ lb. rhubarb

Generous pinch of cinnamon

2 tsp. gelatin

2 oz. bittersweet chocolate

1 cup whipping cream

1 tbs. chopped pistachios

Quickly knead the flour, ⅓ cup sugar, the vanilla, 1 pinch of salt, the egg yolk and butter into a smooth tart pastry. Chill 1 hour. • Wash and clean the rhubarb, removing the strings, and cut into small pieces. Simmer 10 minutes with the remaining sugar, 1 pinch of salt and the cinnamon in 3 tablespoons water. • Dissolve the gelatin in a little cold water and stir into the rhubarb. Allow to cool. • Preheat the oven to 425°. Roll out the dough to a sheet ⅛ inch thick. Use it to line the tart pans. Prick the bottoms well with a fork. • Bake the tart shells 20 minutes until light brown. • Melt the chocolate in a bowl set in hot water and brush it onto the tart shells. Whip the cream until stiff and fold into the rhubarb, then spoon into the tart shells. Sprinkle with the pistachios.

## Strawberry-Almond Tartlets

### Quick and easy to make

Preparation time: 1½ hours
Baking time: 15-20 minutes

| Ingredients for 12 tart pans |
| --- |
| 2 cups flour |
| 1 tsp. baking powder |
| 1¼ cups ground almonds |
| ⅔ cup butter |
| ⅔ cup sugar |
| Pinch of salt |
| 1 egg yolk |
| 1⅔ lbs. strawberries |
| 2 oz. bittersweet chocolate |
| 1 tbs. raspberry liqueur |
| ¾ cup whipping cream |
| 5 tbs. strawberry jam |
| 1 tbs. chopped pistachios |

Quickly knead the flour with the baking powder, almonds, butter cut in pieces, the sugar, salt and egg yolk to a smooth pastry dough and chill 1 hour. • Preheat the oven to 350°. • Wash and pat the strawberries dry and remove the stems. Halve the larger berries. • Roll out the dough to a thin sheet and use it to line the buttered tart pans. Bake 15 to 20 minutes until golden brown. • Melt the chocolate in a bowl set in hot water and stir into the liqueur and whipping cream. Brush the tarts with the cooled chocolate. Fill with strawberries and glaze with the jam. Press the whipped cream from a pastry bag onto the tartlets and sprinkle with the pistachios.

## Meringues with Strawberries

### Requires some time, easy to make

Preparation time: 30 minutes
Baking time: 2 hours

| Ingredients for 8 tartlets |
| --- |
| 3 egg whites |
| 1¼ cups plus 1 tbs. superfine sugar |
| ½ tsp. lemon juice |
| 1 lb. small strawberries |
| ¾ oz. bittersweet chocolate |
| 1 cup whipping cream |
| ½ tsp. vanilla |

In a bowl free of any trace of shortening, beat the egg whites so stiff that a knife drawn through them leaves a visible cut. Dribble in three-quarters of the sugar a little at a time, add the lemon juice and whip until the sugar has dissolved and the egg whites stand in peaks. Whip in the remaining sugar. • Line a baking sheet with waxed or brown paper and mark 8 3-inch circles with a pencil. Put the meringue in a pastry bag fitted with a flower tip and pipe 8 tight spirals onto the paper, beginning at the center. Around the rim pipe a ring of kisses (small mounds). Set the pan on the middle rack of the oven. Turn the heat to 200° and bake, or rather dry, the meringues 2 hours. • Remove the tartlets from the paper. • Wash and drain the strawberries and remove the stems. Grate the chocolate. Whip the cream with the vanilla until stiff and fold in the chocolate. Put the mixture in a pastry bag fitted with a flower tip and pipe into the tartlets. Halve the strawberries and arrange in a rosette shape on the cream.

## Raspberry Tartlets with Pistachio Cream

**Easy to make**

Preparation time: 20 minutes
Baking time: 20 minutes
Time to put the tarts together:
30 minutes

Ingredients for 8 tartlets

1 cup ricotta or cottage cheese

5 tbs. milk

5 tbs. vegetable oil

⅔ cup sugar

½ tsp. vanilla

Pinch of salt

2 cups flour

3 tsp. baking powder

1 tsp. gelatin

1 egg yolk

¾ cup whipping cream

1 lb. raspberries

2 tbs. chopped pistachios

Drain the cheese. Combine half the cheese with the milk, oil, ⅓ cup of the sugar, the vanilla and salt. Stir until smooth. Knead the flour and baking powder into the cheese mixture and roll out ¼ inch thick. Cut out 8 4-inch circles. • Preheat the oven to 400°. Bake the tartlets 20 minutes on a greased baking sheet until golden brown. • Dissolve the gelatin in a little water. Beat the egg yolk with the remaining sugar until lemon colored. Add the remaining cheese. Heat the gelatin water, add 2 tablespoons of the cheese mixture, stir and return to the cheese. • Whip the cream until stiff and fold half into the cheese. Spread this on the cooled pastry cut-outs. Cover with raspberries. Put the remaining cream in a pastry bag and pipe decorations around the raspberries. Sprinkle with pistachios.

## Tartlets with Red Currants

**Nutritious, easy to make**

Preparation time: 25 minutes
Baking time: 15-20 minutes
Time to put the tartlets together:
20 minutes

Ingredients for 8 tart pans:

1½ cups plus 1 tbs. whole-wheat flour

3 tbs. buckwheat flour

3 tbs. millet flour

1 tsp. baking powder

Generous pinch cinnamon

¾ cup butter

¾ cup plus 2 tbs. honey

1 egg

¼ lb. red currants

¾ cup whipping cream

Knead the flour, baking powder, cinnamon, ½ cup flaked butter, ½ of the honey and the egg. Let stand 15 minutes. • Preheat the oven to 400°. Butter the tart pans. • Divide the dough into 8 equal pieces, shape balls and roll out. Line the tart pans and cut off excess dough. • Bake the tart shells 15 to 20 minutes or until golden brown. • Wash the currants and remove the stems. Mix the remaining butter with the remaining honey until smooth. Stir in the berries, reserving some for garnish. Whip the cream until stiff and add three-quarters of the cream to the berries. • Fill the tart shells with the berries and cream. Garnish with the remaining berries and small mounds of whipped cream.

## Orange Cakes

### Inexpensive and easy to make

Preparation time: 40 minutes
Baking time: 20 minutes

| Ingredients for 1 jelly roll pan |
| --- |
| ¾ cup plus 2 tbs. butter |
| 1 cup sugar |
| ½ tsp. vanilla |
| Pinch of salt |
| 3 eggs |
| 2 cups flour |
| 2 tsp. baking powder |
| 1 lemon |
| 1 orange |
| 1⅓ cups powdered sugar |

Cream the butter and add the sugar, vanilla, salt and eggs a little at a time. Mix the flour with the baking powder. Wash the lemon in lukewarm water. Grate the rind and squeeze the lemon. Mix the rind with the flour and add to the first mixture with the lemon juice. • Preheat the oven to 350° and generously butter the jelly roll pan. • Spread the batter over ¾ of the pan, using a strip of folded aluminum foil to keep the batter from spreading. • Bake 20 minutes on the middle rack until pale yellow. • Wash the orange in lukewarm water. Dry and grate the rind and squeeze the orange. Stir the powdered sugar into the orange juice. • Brush the cake with the juice while still warm and sprinkle with grated orange rind. Allow the glaze to dry. • Cut the cake into 24 narrow rectangles.

## Berry Boatlets

### Requires some time

Preparation time: 10 minutes
Chilling time: 1 hour
Baking time: 15-20 minutes
Time to put the boatlets together: 1 hour

| Ingredients for 12 boatlet pans |
| --- |
| For the tart pastry: |
| 2 cups flour |
| ⅔ cup powdered sugar |
| ⅔ cup ground almonds |
| 7 tbs. butter |
| 1 egg yolk |
| For the filling: |
| ¼ lb. raspberries |
| ½ cup milk |
| 1 heaping tsp. cornstarch |
| 1½ tbs. sugar |
| 2 egg yolks |
| ½ vanilla bean |
| ¼ cup egg wash |
| ½ cup whipping cream |

Quickly knead the tart pastry ingredients into a smooth dough. Cover and chill 1 hour. • Wash and pat the berries dry. • Preheat the oven to 350°. Roll the dough out thinly. Butter the tart pans and line them with the dough. Bake 15 to 20 minutes on the middle rack of the oven. • Bring the milk to a boil. Stir the cornstarch with a tablespoon of cold water, add 1 tablespoon of the sugar and stir into the milk. Bring to a boil, remove from the heat and stir in the egg yolks. Slit the vanilla bean open and scrape out the soft center. Stir into the milk mixture with the egg wash. Allow to cool. • Whip the cream until stiff with the remaining sugar. • Fill the boatlets with the custard and berries and top with small mounds of whipped cream.

# Grape Tartlets

**Requires some time**

Preparation time: 1¾ hours
Baking time: 20 minutes

| Ingredients for 8 tart pans |
| --- |
| For the pastry dough: |
| 2⅓ cups flour |
| ⅔ cup butter |
| ⅔ cup sugar |
| ½ tsp. vanilla |
| Pinch of salt |
| 1 egg |
| For the filling: |
| ½ tbs. gelatin |
| 3 eggs |
| ⅔ cup powdered sugar |
| ½ cup Marsala wine |
| 2 tbs. lemon juice |
| ¾ lb. red grapes |
| ¾ lb. green grapes |
| ⅔ cup sliced almonds |

Quickly knead the ingredients for the tart pastry. Chill 1 hour. • Dissolve the gelatin in a little cold water. Separate the eggs. In a saucepan heat some water to just under a boil. Set a small mixing bowl in the pan, add the egg yolks and powdered sugar and beat until lemon colored. Add the wine. Heat the lemon juice, add the dissolved gelatin and stir into the egg-sugar mixture. Beat the egg whites until stiff and fold into the first mixture with the whisk. Chill 1 hour to stiffen, stirring occasionally. • Preheat the oven to 400°. Butter the tart pans well. Divide the dough into 8 pieces and roll out. Line the pans with the dough. Prick the bottoms well with a fork and cut off the edges. Bake 20 minutes until golden brown. • Wash and pat the grapes dry and remove the stems. • Pour the wine custard into the tart shells. Fill with grapes and sprinkle sliced almonds around the edges.

# Baking Pan Cakes

## Old-Fashioned Beehive Cake

**Requires some time**

Preparation time: 30 minutes
Baking time: 30 minutes
Time to put the cake together:
20 minutes

Ingredients for 1 jelly roll pan
2 tsp. dry yeast
⅓ cup plus 2 tbs. sugar
1 cup lukewarm milk
3¾ cups plus 1 tbs. flour
3½ tbs. softened butter
Pinch of salt
For the almond crust:
7 tbs. melted butter
2½ cups sliced almonds
1 cup sugar
3 tbs. milk
For the custard:
2 tsp. gelatin
2 cups milk
1 egg
⅓ cup plus 2 tbs. sugar
½ tsp. vanilla
⅓ cup cornstarch

**W**hisk the yeast with a little of the sugar and milk and set aside 15 minutes to form the sponge. • Mix in the flour, butter, remaining sugar and salt and knead well. Let rise 30 minutes. • Mix the butter, almonds, sugar and milk. • Roll out the dough on a lightly greased jelly roll pan. Spread the almond mixture on top and let rise 15 minutes longer. • Preheat the oven to 400°. • Bake the cake 30 minutes. • Dissolve the gelatin in a little water. Make a custard from the remaining ingredients except for the egg. Add the egg yolk and dissolved gelatin. Beat the egg white and fold in. • Cut the cake into four pieces, slice each into two layers and fill with the custard. Cut into quarters.

## Beehive Cake with Honey

**Nutritious**

Preparation time: 30 minutes
Rising time: 1 hour
Baking time: 25 minutes
Time to put the cake together:
30 minutes

Ingredients for 1 jelly roll pan
For the dough:
4⅔ cups whole-wheat flour
⅓ cup plus 1 tbs. soy flour
½ tsp. cinnamon
2 tsp. dry yeast
1½ cups warm milk
3 tbs. honey
3½ tbs. softened butter
For the almond crust:
2½ cups sliced almonds
¾ cup honey
7 tbs. butter
For the custard:
¼ cup honey
2 cups milk
¼ cup cornstarch or arrowroot
½ tsp. vanilla
1 cup plus 2 tbs. softened butter

**M**ix the flours with the cinnamon. Make a well and add the yeast, milk and honey and stir with some of the flour. Allow the sponge to form 15 minutes. • Knead the dough with the butter and let rise 30 minutes. • Roll out on the greased jelly roll pan and let rise 15 minutes longer. • Heat the almonds with the honey and butter and spread on the dough. • Preheat the oven to 425°. Bake the cake 25 minutes. • Heat the honey. Whisk the milk with the cornstarch and vanilla. Pour into the honey, bring to a boil and allow to cool. Stir it into the butter 1 tablespoon at a time. • Prepare the cake as described in the previous recipe.

## Marble Cake with Poppy Seed

**Nutritious**

Preparation time: 45 minutes
Baking time: 1 hour

Ingredients for a 10-inch loaf pan

2⅓ cups whole-wheat flour

2 tsp. baking powder

½ tsp. vanilla

¾ cup plus 2 tbs. softened butter

¾ cup honey

4 eggs

3½ tbs. diced citron

1 cup ground poppy seed

1 tbs. rose water

½ tsp. cinnamon

2 tsp. cocoa

2 tbs. rum

2 tbs. lemon juice

Mix the flour with the baking powder. Cream the butter with the vanilla and ⅔ cup of the honey. Stir in the eggs and the flour alternately a little at a time. Add the citron. • Preheat the oven to 350°. Butter the pan well and pour in half the batter. With the remaining batter mix the poppy seed, rose water, cinnamon, cocoa and the remaining honey. Spread the dark batter on the light and pull a fork through both in a circular motion. • Bake the marble cake 1 hour on the middle rack of the oven. Turn off the heat and leave the cake in the oven 5 minutes longer. • Mix the rum with the lemon juice and pour over the cake. Cool in the pan. • After 2 days the aroma will have fully developed.

## Classic Marble Cake

**Famous recipe**

Preparation time: 30 minutes
Baking time: 1 hour

Ingredients for 1 bundt pan

1 cup plus 2 tbs. butter

1½ cups sugar

½ tsp. vanilla

4 eggs

3 cups plus 1 tbs. flour

⅔ cup cornstarch

1 tbs. baking powder

Pinch of salt

½ cup milk

3 tbs. cocoa

1 tbs. powdered sugar

Cream the butter and gradually add the sugar and vanilla. Add the eggs one at a time. Mix the flour with the cornstarch, baking powder and salt and add alternately with the milk to the first mixture. • Preheat the oven to 350°. Butter the pan well. • Pour half the batter into the pan. Mix the cocoa with the remaining batter and spread the dark batter on the light. Pull a fork through both batters in a circular motion to produce the "marbling" effect. • Bake 1 hour on the middle rack of the oven. Use a toothpick to test. (If the dough sticks to the toothpick the cake will need to bake a few minutes longer.) • Turn the cake out of the pan when somewhat cool and dust with powdered sugar.

## Panettone

### Italian specialty

Preparation time: 30 minutes
Rising time: 1¼ hours
Baking time: 1½ hours

| Ingredients for 1 panettone pan or a 2 quart pot |
| --- |
| 2 tsp. dry yeast |
| ¾ cup sugar |
| ½ cup lukewarm milk |
| 3¾ cups plus 1 tbs. flour |
| 4 egg yolks |
| ½ tsp. vanilla |
| Grated rind of 1 lemon |
| ½ tsp. salt |
| ½ cup plus 1 tbs. butter |
| ⅔ cup raisins |
| ⅔ cup diced candied citron |
| 3 tbs. candied orange rind |
| ⅔ cup sliced almonds |

Dissolve the yeast with 1 teaspoon of the sugar in the milk. Set aside 15 minutes to develop the sponge. • Knead the flour with the yeast, the remaining sugar, the egg yolks, vanilla, lemon rind, salt. Add the butter. Knead the dough 5 minutes longer, adding some flour if necessary. Let it rise again for 30 minutes. • Wash the raisins in hot water, pat them dry and knead into the dough with the citron, candied orange and almonds. Let rise 20 minutes longer. • Line the pan with waxed paper or aluminum foil or spread with butter. Allow the dough to rise once more in the pan. • Preheat the oven to 400°. Brush the surface of the dough with melted butter and score a cross in the top with a knife. • Bake 1½ hours on the bottom rack of the oven.

## English Cake

### Famous recipe

Preparation time: 30 minutes
Baking time: 1¼ hours

| Ingredients for a 12-inch loaf pan |
| --- |
| 1 cup plus 2 tbs. butter |
| 4 eggs |
| 1½ cups sugar |
| 1 vanilla bean |
| 2 tbs. rum |
| ⅓ cup candied citron |
| ⅓ cup candied orange rind |
| Grated rind of ½ lemon |
| 2 tbs. lemon juice |
| Pinch of salt |
| 1 cup raisins |
| 2 cups flour |
| ¾ cup plus 1 tbs. cornstarch |
| 2 tsp. baking powder |
| ⅔ cup sliced almonds |
| ⅔ cup bread crumbs |
| ⅔ cup powdered sugar |
| 2 tbs. lemon juice |

Cream the butter. Separate the eggs. Beat the sugar into the butter little by little and the eggs one at a time. Beat the egg whites until stiff. Slit open the vanilla bean, scrape out the soft center and stir into the batter with the rum. Dice the citron and orange rind and add with the lemon rind, lemon juice and salt. Wash the raisins in hot water and drain. Mix the flour with the cornstarch and baking powder and add to the batter alternately with the whipped egg whites. Add the raisins and almonds. • Preheat the oven to 350°. Butter the pan well and sprinkle with bread crumbs. Pour the batter into the pan and bake 60 to 75 minutes on the lower rack of the oven. • Stir the powdered sugar and lemon juice to make a glaze. Pour over the baked cake.

# Savarin

### A French specialty

Preparation time: 20 minutes
Rising time: 1 hour
Baking time: 40 minutes
Time to put the cake together:
about 30 minutes each

For the dough:

| |
|---|
| 1½ tsp. dry yeast |
| ⅓ cup sugar |
| ½ cup lukewarm milk |
| ½ cup plus 1 tbs. butter |
| ½ tsp. vanilla |
| Salt |
| 4 eggs |
| 2⅔ cups flour |
| For the peach Savarin: |
| 1⅔ lbs. peaches |
| 1 cup peach juice |
| Juice of 1 lemon |
| ¼ cup apricot brandy |
| ½ cup whipping cream |
| 1 tbs. egg wash |

| |
|---|
| 1 tbs. chopped pistachios |
| For the lingonberry Savarin: |
| ⅔ cup plus 1 tsp. sugar |
| ½ cup Madeira |
| ½ cup water |
| ⅔ cup apricot marmalade |
| ½ vanilla bean |
| ½ cup whipping cream |
| 1½ cups lingonberry jam |
| For the orange Savarin: |
| 6 oranges |
| 5 tbs. Cointreau |
| Juice of 1 lemon |
| 6 tbs. light rum |
| ⅓ cup plus 2 tbs. sugar |
| ½ cup water |
| ⅔ cup orange marmalade |
| ½ cup whipping cream |
| 1 oz. chocolate |

**S**ir the yeast with 1 teaspoon of the sugar and a little of the milk. Cover and let stand 15 minutes to form the sponge. • Whisk the butter with the re-

maining sugar, the vanilla, salt, remaining milk and the eggs. Mix with the flour and yeast sponge and knead well. Cover and let rise 30 minutes. Set in the buttered mold and let rise 15 minutes longer. • Preheat the oven to 400°. Bake 30 minutes on the lower rack of the oven. • For the peach Savarin, dip the fruit in boiling water, remove skins and pits and cut into eighths. Bring the fruit juices and the apricot brandy to a boil. • Pour the juice into the Savarin mold. Set the baked Savarin in the mold and turn it out when the juice has been absorbed. • Whip the cream with the egg wash until stiff. Fill the Savarin with the peach slices and top with the whipped cream. Sprinkle with the pistachios. • For the lingonberry Savarin, caramelize ⅔ cup of the sugar, then add the Madeira and water. Pour the liquid into the Savarin mold, set in

the baked Savarin and turn it out of the mold when all the juice has been absorbed. Brush with the heated apricot marmalade. Scrape the soft center out of the vanilla bean, add to the cream with the remaining sugar and whip the cream until stiff. • For the orange Savarin, peel 4 of the oranges, removing the rind and the white skin. Cut into slices, quarter the slices and douse with Cointreau. Squeeze the juice from the other oranges and mix with the lemon juice, rum, sugar and water. Bring to a boil, pour into the Savarin mold, set the baked Savarin in the mold to absorb the liquid. Heat the jam, press through a sieve and brush on the Savarin. Whip the cream until stiff. Grate the chocolate and fold into the whipped cream. Fill the Savarin with the orange slices and top with whipped cream.

## Chestnut Cake

### Somewhat difficult

Preparation time: 1 hour
Baking time: 1 hour

| Ingredients for a 9-inch springform pan |
| --- |
| For the tart pastry: |
| 1½ cups plus 1 tbs. flour |
| 7 tbs. butter |
| ½ cup powdered sugar |
| 1 egg yolk |
| For the filling: |
| 1⅔ lbs. unshelled chestnuts |
| ⅔ cup softened butter |
| 1 cup sugar |
| ½ tsp. vanilla |
| 1 tsp. cinnamon |
| 2 eggs |
| 2 egg whites |
| For flavoring: |
| 2 tbs. amaretto |

**W**ith cold hands quickly knead the flour with the butter, powdered sugar and egg yolk into a smooth dough. Cover and chill 1 hour. • Preheat the oven to 400°. • Cut a cross in the pointed end of the chestnuts and roast 10 minutes in the oven. • When they are somewhat cool peel the chestnuts and remove the brown skin under the shell. Bring a little water to a boil in a saucepan and boil the chestnuts 20 minutes. • Cream the butter with the sugar, vanilla and cinnamon. Separate the eggs. Mix the egg yolks with the butter-sugar mixture and beat the egg whites until stiff. • Drain the chestnuts, allow them to cool somewhat, then puree in a food processor. Add to the butter-sugar mixture with the egg whites. • Preheat the oven to 350°. • Line the pan with the rolled-out pastry dough, shaping 1-inch sides. Bake 10 minutes. Fill with the chestnut mixture and bake 50 minutes. • Sprinkle the cake with the amaretto. Serve with chilled, sweetened whipped cream.

# King's Cake

**Nutritious, easy to make**

Preparation time: 45 minutes
Baking time: 70 minutes

Ingredients for an 11-inch loaf pan

3 cups plus 1 tbs. whole-wheat flour

2 tsp. baking powder

½ tsp. vanilla

Grated rind of 1 lemon

¾ cup plus 1 tbs. butter

¾ cup honey

4 eggs

3 tbs. rum

⅔ cup raisins

⅓ cup currants

⅓ cup diced candied citron

⅓ cup diced candied orange rind

**M**ix the flour with the baking powder, vanilla and lemon rind. Cream the butter with the honey and add the eggs, rum and flour alternately, a little at a time. Stir well. • Wash the raisins and currants in hot water, pat dry and add to the batter with the citron and orange rind. Let stand about 30 minutes. • Preheat the oven to 350°. Butter the pan well. • Spread the batter evenly in the pan and bake 70 minutes on the middle rack of the oven. Test with a toothpick. If some dough clings to the toothpick the cake needs another 10 minutes in the oven. • Allow the cake to cool in the pan. • King's Cake develops its full aroma in one day and will stay fresh, if kept cool in a tightly closed container, for one week.

# Kaiser Cake

**Nutritious**

Preparation time: 1 hour
Baking time: 50 minutes

Ingredients for an 11-inch springform pan

1 cup pitted prunes

1 cup whole walnuts

½ cup diced candied citron

5 tbs. Armagnac

3 cups plus 1 tbs. whole-wheat flour

2 tsp. baking powder

⅛ tsp. vanilla

7 eggs

½ cup plus 1 tbs. cold butter

½ cup honey

⅔ cup unrefined granulated cane sugar

3½ tbs. melted butter

**F**inely dice the prunes and nuts and mix with the citron and Armagnac. • Mix 2 cups of the flour with 1 teaspoon of the baking powder and the vanilla. Separate the eggs. Knead 1 egg yolk with the flaked butter, the honey and flour mixture. Chill the dough. • Beat the remaining egg yolks with the unrefined sugar and 2 tablespoons warm water. Add the remaining flour and baking powder and mix well. Beat the egg whites until stiff and fold in. • Preheat the oven to 350°. Butter the pan. • Line the pan with the thinly rolled-out pastry dough shaping 1-inch sides. Mix the brandy-soaked fruit and melted butter with the cake batter and pour into the pan. From the leftover pastry dough make a lattice design over the sponge cake. • Bake 50 minutes.

## Arrack Cake

**Nutritious, easy to make**

Preparation time: 30 minutes
Baking time: 50 minutes

Ingredients for a 9-inch loaf pan

1½ cups plus 1 tbs. whole-wheat flour

3 tbs. flour

½ cup cocoa

2 tsp. baking powder

½ tsp. cinnamon

½ tsp. ginger

1 orange

2 tbs. unrefined granulated cane sugar

⅔ cup softened butter

⅔ cup plus 1 tbs. honey

3 eggs

¼ cup arrack

**M**ix the flours with the cocoa, baking powder, cinnamon and ginger. Wash the orange in warm water, dry and grate the rind. Add the rind with the unrefined sugar to the dry ingredients. • Cream the butter with ½ cup honey. Add the eggs, 2 tablespoons of the arrack and the flour alternately, a little at a time. • Preheat the oven to 350°. Butter the pan well. • Pour the batter in the pan and spread evenly. Bake about 50 minutes on the lower rack of the oven. Test with a toothpick. • Turn off the heat and leave the cake in the oven 10 minutes longer. • Squeeze the juice from the orange and mix with the remaining honey and arrack. • Pour the juice mixture over the cake and cool in the pan. • Arrack cake tastes best after standing 1 day and stays fresh 2 to 3 days after baking.

## Spice Cake

**Easy to make, inexpensive**

Preparation time: 20 minutes
Baking time: 1 hour

Ingredients for a 12-inch loaf pan

⅔ cup bread crumbs

¾ cup plus 1 tbs. softened butter

1½ cups sugar

1 tsp. vanilla

4 eggs

1¾ cups ground hazelnuts

1 tsp. cinnamon

Generous pinch of ground cloves

Generous pinch of ground ginger

2 cups flour

3 tsp. baking powder

2 tbs. rum

**P**reheat the oven to 400°. Butter the pan and sprinkle with bread crumbs. • Cream the butter with the sugar and vanilla. Add the eggs, ground nuts and spices a little at a time. Mix the flour with the baking powder and add to the batter with the rum 1 tablespoon at a time. • Pour the batter into the pan, spread evenly and bake 1 hour on the middle rack of the oven. • The spice cake should stand 1 day before being cut in order to develop its full aroma.

Tip: Instead of the hazelnuts use ground almonds. Instead of ginger try cardamom and/or nutmeg. Spice cake is an ideal cake to bake ahead. If it is not cut it can be kept in a tightly closed container or wrapped in aluminum foil for 2 weeks.

# Marbled Orange Cake

**Nutritious**

Preparation time: 45 minutes
Baking time: 1 hour

Ingredients for a 10-inch loaf pan

2 cups whole-wheat flour

2 tsp. baking powder

½ tsp. vanilla

⅔ cup softened butter

¾ cup plus 1 tbs. honey

4 eggs

1 cup hazelnuts

⅔ cup blanched almonds

1 orange

2 tsp. cocoa

2 tbs. Cointreau

**M**ix the flour with the baking powder and the vanilla. Cream the butter with ⅓ cup of the honey. Mix in 3 of the eggs and the flour alternately a little at a time. • Preheat the oven to 350°. Butter the pan well. • Pour the batter into the pan and spread evenly. • Finely grind the hazelnuts and the almonds. Wash the orange in hot water, dry it and grate the rind. Add the rind to the cocoa, the remaining honey and egg and beat well. Spread the nut mixture on the dough and stir briefly with a fork. • Bake the cake about 1 hour on the middle rack of the oven, then test with a toothpick or thin wooden skewer. • Turn the heat off and leave the cake in the oven 5 minutes longer. • Squeeze the juice from the orange and stir with the Cointreau. Brush the cake evenly with the juice mixture and allow to cool in the pan. • If put in a tightly closed container and chilled, the orange cake will stay fresh for about 1 week.

# French Orange Cake

**Quick and easy to make**

Preparation time: 30 minutes
Baking time: 50 minutes
Time to put the cake together: 10 minutes

Ingredients for a 10-inch springform pan

4 eggs

1 cup plus 1 tbs. sugar

1 orange

½ cup plus 1 tbs. flour

½ cup plus 1 tbs. cornstarch

½ tsp. baking powder

⅓ cup melted butter

½ cup sliced almonds

1 scant cup orange juice, freshly squeezed

Juice of 1 lemon

1 tbs. sugar

2 tbs. powdered sugar

**S**eparate the eggs. Cream the egg yolks with the sugar. • Wash the orange in hot water and grate the rind. Mix with the flour, cornstarch and baking powder and add to the egg-sugar mixture. Beat the egg whites until stiff and fold into the dough. • Preheat the oven to 350°. Grease only the bottom of the pan, cover it with waxed paper, butter the paper and sprinkle with the almonds. • Pour the batter into the pan and spread evenly. Bake the cake 50 minutes or until golden brown. Turn off the heat and leave in the oven 10 minutes longer. • Pour the orange juice through a sieve and mix with the lemon juice and sugar. Warm the juices. • Turn the cake out of the pan and remove the paper. Poke holes in the cake with a toothpick and soak with the warm juice. • Shortly before serving sift the powdered sugar over the cake.

## Chocolate Streusel Cake

### Quick and easy to make

Preparation time: 40 minutes
Baking time: 50 minutes

Ingredients for a 10-inch springform pan

⅓ cup butter

⅓ cup plus 2 tbs. sugar

½ tsp. vanilla

1 egg

Grated rind of 1 lemon

Juice of ½ lemon

1¼ cups flour

⅓ cup plus 1 tbs. cornstarch

2 tsp. baking powder

3-4 tbs. milk

3 tbs. apricot marmalade

1 lb. fully ripe apricots

1¼ cups flour

½ cup cocoa

⅔ cup sugar

½ tsp. vanilla

7 tbs. softened butter

1 tbs. powdered sugar

Cream the butter. Add the sugar, vanilla, egg, lemon rind and lemon juice. Mix the flour with the cornstarch and baking powder. Add the milk and stir into the first mixture. • Butter the pan and line with the dough. • Stir the apricot marmalade with 1 tablespoon hot water until smooth and spread on the dough. Wash, dry, halve and pit the apricots and arrange on the dough. • Preheat the oven to 400°. • To make the streusel, combine all the remaining ingredients except for the powdered sugar. Sprinkle the streusel over the fruit. • Bake the cake 50 minutes, turn off the heat and leave in the oven 10 minutes longer. • Sift powdered sugar over the cooled cake.

## Streusel Cake with Cheese Custard

### Requires some time

Preparation time: 50 minutes
Rising time: 1 hour
Baking time: 30 minutes

Ingredients for 1 jelly roll pan

2 tsp. dry yeast

⅓ cup plus 2 tbs. sugar

1 cup milk

3¾ cups plus 1 tbs. flour

⅓ cup softened butter

Pinch of salt

2 eggs

2 cups low-fat ricotta or cottage cheese

⅔ cup sugar

2½ tbs. cornstarch

½ cup raisins

1½ cups plus 1 tbs. flour

¼ cup plus 2 tbs. ground almonds

⅔ cup sugar

⅔ cup butter

Stir the yeast with 1 teaspoon of the sugar and some of the milk. Set aside 15 minutes to form the sponge. • Put 2 cups of flour in a bowl with the yeast sponge, the remaining milk and sugar, the butter and salt. Knead in the rest of the flour, adding flour as needed. Cover and let rise 45 minutes. • Separate the eggs. Mix the egg yolks with the cheese, sugar, and cornstarch. Beat the egg whites until stiff and add to the cheese mixture with raisins. • Thoroughly knead the dough once more and roll out on the greased pan. Spread with the cheese mixture. • Preheat the oven to 400°. • Mix the flour with the almonds, sugar and butter to make the streusel and sprinkle it over the cake. • Bake the cake 30 minutes, turn off the heat and leave the cake in the oven 10 minutes longer.

## Poppy Seed Cake with Streusel

### Easy to make

Preparation time: 1 hour
Baking time: 45 minutes

| Ingredients for 1 jelly roll pan |
| --- |
| 1¾ cups ground poppy seeds |
| 1½ cups milk |
| ⅔ cup sugar |
| Grated rind of 1 lemon |
| 2 tbs. butter |
| 1 egg |
| ⅓ cup cornstarch |
| 4 oz. almond paste |
| For the streusel: |
| ¾ cup plus 1 tbs. butter |
| 2 cups flour |
| ½ cup blanched almonds |
| 1¼ cups plus 1 tbs. sugar |
| Pinch of salt |
| ½ tsp. cinnamon |
| For the dough: |
| ⅔ cup ricotta or cottage cheese |
| 5 tbs. milk |
| 6 tbs. vegetable oil |
| ⅓ cup plus 2 tbs. sugar |
| Pinch of salt |
| ½ tsp. vanilla |
| 2⅓ cups flour |
| 1 tbs. baking powder |

**M**ix the poppy seed with 1 cup of the milk, the sugar, lemon rind and butter. Bring to a boil and cook 10 minutes over low heat. • Separate the egg. Stir the cornstarch with the egg yolk and remaining milk and add to the poppy seed mixture. Bring to a boil and turn off the heat. • Dice the almond paste, mix to a smooth paste with the egg white and stir into the poppy seed mixture. Allow to cool. • To make the streusel, mix all the streusel ingredients together and crumble. • Butter a baking pan well and preheat the oven to 400°. • To make the dough, combine the cheese, milk, oil, sugar, salt, vanilla and half the flour. Mix well. Mix the remaining flour with the baking powder and knead in. • Roll out the cheese dough in the

jelly roll pan, pulling the edges up somewhat. Spread with the poppy seed mixture and sprinkle with the streusel. • Bake 45 minutes until golden brown. Turn off the heat and leave the cake in the oven 10 minutes longer.

## Marzipan-Almond Slices

**Somewhat expensive, quick to make**

Preparation time: 45 minutes
Baking time: 30 minutes

| Ingredients for 1 jelly roll pan |
| --- |
| For the dough: |
| ⅔ cup butter |
| 6 eggs |
| 1½ cups sugar |
| Pinch of salt |
| Grated rind of 1 lemon |
| 2⅔ cups flour |
| 1 tbs. baking powder |

| |
| --- |
| 6 tbs. milk |
| For the topping: |
| ⅔ cup butter |
| ⅓ cup plus 1 tbs. crème fraîche |
| 1 cup sugar |
| Salt |
| ½ tsp. vanilla |
| 7 oz. almond paste |
| 2 tbs. cognac |
| 4 cups sliced almonds |

**M**elt the butter and cool. Beat the eggs with the sugar, salt and lemon rind until lemon colored. Stir in the butter, flour, baking powder and milk. • Preheat the oven to 400°. • Butter the jelly roll pan. Pour in the batter and spread evenly. Bake 15 minutes. • Bring the butter, crème fraîche, sugar, salt and vanilla to a boil and remove from the heat. Dice the almond paste and mix with the cognac. Stir in the butter-sugar mixture and fold in the sliced almonds. •

Spread the almond mixture on the cake and bake 15 minutes longer. • Cut the cooled cake into 24 pieces.

## White Wine Cake

### Quick and easy to make

Preparation time: 15 minutes
Baking time: 45 minutes
Time to put the cake together: 10 minutes

| Ingredients for a 9-inch springform pan |
| --- |
| ⅔ cup bread crumbs |
| ⅔ cup butter |
| 1¼ cups plus 1 tbs. sugar |
| 1 tsp. vanilla |
| 3 eggs |
| Pinch of salt |
| Grated rind of 1 lemon |
| 2⅓ cups flour |
| ⅓ cup plus 1 tbs. cornstarch |
| 3 tsp. baking powder |
| ¾ cup white wine |

| |
| --- |
| 3 tbs. white rum |
| For the glaze: |
| 1½ cups powdered sugar |
| 3 tbs. lemon juice |

**P**reheat the oven to 350°. Butter the pan and sprinkle with bread crumbs. • Cream the butter with the sugar and vanilla. Beat in the eggs, one at a time and add the salt. Wash the lemon in warm water, cut in half and squeeze the juice. Grate the lemon rind and beat with the juice into the batter. Mix the flour with the cornstarch and baking powder. Stir into the batter with half the white wine and the rum 1 tablespoon at a time. • Pour the batter into the pan and bake 45 minutes on the lower rack of the oven. • Prick the cake well with a toothpick and sprinkle with the remaining wine. Allow to cool somewhat. • Pour the glaze over the cake and garnish as desired.

## Speckled Egg Cake

### Famous recipe

Preparation time: 40 minutes
Rising time: 1 hour
Baking time: 45 minutes

| Ingredients for 1 jelly roll pan |
| --- |
| For the dough: |
| 3¾ cups plus 1 tbs. flour |
| 2 tsp. dry yeast |
| ⅔ cup sugar |
| 1 scant cup lukewarm milk |
| 7 tbs. softened butter |
| Pinch of salt |
| For the topping: |
| 7 eggs |
| ½ cup butter |
| ⅔ cup sugar |
| 1 tsp. vanilla |
| 1¼ cups ricotta or cottage cheese |
| ⅓ cup cornstarch |
| 1 cup raisins |
| 1 cup sliced almonds |
| Grated rind of ½ lemon |

Sift the flour into a bowl, make a well in the middle and add the yeast into it with 1 teaspoon of the sugar and a little milk. Stir together with a little of the flour. Cover and set aside 15 minutes for the sponge to form. • Knead the butter, salt, remaining sugar and flour with the yeast sponge. Cover and let rise 30 minutes. • Roll out the dough and place in the buttered pan. • Preheat the oven to 400°. • Separate the eggs. Cream the butter with the sugar and vanilla. Add the egg yolks, cheese and cornstarch a little at a time. Wash the raisins in hot water and pat dry. Beat the egg whites until stiff. Mix ½ cup of the sliced almonds, the raisins and the lemon rind with the cheese mixture and fold in the egg whites. • Spread the mixture evenly on the dough and sprinkle with the remaining sliced almonds. Bake 45 minutes on the lower rack of the oven until golden brown.

## Filled Nut Ring

### Easy to make

Preparation time: 40 minutes
Baking time: 50 minutes

| Ingredients for 1 ring |
| --- |
| For the dough: |
| 1 cup ricotta or cottage cheese |
| 6 tbs. milk |
| 1 egg |
| ½ cup vegetable oil |
| ⅔ cup sugar |
| ½ tsp. vanilla |
| Pinch of salt |
| 3¼ cups flour |
| 1 tbs. baking powder |
| For the filling: |
| ½ cup candied orange rind |
| 2 cups chopped hazelnuts |
| Grated rind of ½ lemon |
| ⅓ cup sugar |
| 5 tbs. whipping cream |
| 4 oz. almond paste |
| 1 egg yolk |

Beat the cheese with the milk, egg, oil, sugar, vanilla and salt. Mix the flour with the baking powder, and stir into the cheese mixture 1 tablespoon at a time. Knead well. • To make the filling, finely dice the orange rind and mix with the nuts, lemon rind, sugar and 4 tablespoons of the cream. Cut the almond paste into thin slices. • Preheat the oven to 350°. Butter a baking sheet. • On a floured surface roll out the dough to a long 8 × 32-inch strip. Lay the slices of almond paste down the center of the strip and cover with the nut mixture. Fold the dough over the filling from both sides and press together. Place the roll on the baking sheet with the seam down, shape a ring and press the ends together well. Whisk the egg yolk with the remaining cream, brush it on the ring and make zig-zag incisions in the dough with kitchen shears. • Bake the nut ring 50 minutes on the middle rack of the oven until golden brown.

# Nut Pound Cake

### Easy to make

Preparation time: 30 minutes
Baking time: 70 minutes

Ingredients for a 12-inch loaf pan

¾ cup softened butter

1½ cups sugar

½ tsp. vanilla

4 eggs

1¼ cups flour

½ cup plus 1 tbs. cornstarch

1 tsp. baking powder

¾ cup plus 1 tbs. ground hazelnuts

½ cup plus 1 tbs. ground walnuts

1 tbs. lemon juice

Cream the butter. Slowly add 1 cup of the sugar with the vanilla. Separate 2 of the eggs. Mix the flour with the cornstarch and baking powder. Beat the 2 egg yolks and 2 whole eggs into the first mixture and add the flour mixture. Preheat the oven to 350°. Line the pan with waxed paper or parchment paper. • Pour the dough into the pan. • Beat the egg whites until stiff and slowly drizzle the remaining sugar in while whipping. Mix in the ground nuts and lemon juice. • Bake 70 minutes on the lower rack of the oven, covering the top lightly with aluminum foil if necessary after the first 45 minutes to avoid excessive browning. • Test with a toothpick. Turn off the heat and leave the cake in the oven 10 minutes longer, then remove from the pan and cool on a cake rack.

# Walliser Nut Cake

### Quick and easy to make

Preparation time: 50 minutes
Baking time: 50 minutes

Ingredients for a 12-inch loaf pan

3 cups shelled walnuts

½ tbs. butter

1¼ cups plus 1 tbs. sugar

1¾ cups shelled hazelnuts

2 oz. (about ¾ cup) zwieback

6 eggs

2 tsp. baking powder

8 oz. chocolate

Reserve 8 walnut halves for garnish. Finely chop 1¼ cups of the walnuts. Heat the butter in a pan, add the chopped walnuts and sauté, stirring constantly. Sprinkle with ½ tablespoon of the sugar to caramelize the walnuts, then remove from the heat and cool. • Grind the remaining nuts in a nut grinder. Crush the zwieback between layers of aluminum foil with a rolling pin. • Line the pan with parchment or waxed paper. Preheat the oven to 350°. • Beat the eggs, and drizzle in the remaining sugar while beating. Add the ground nuts. Mix the zwieback flour with the baking powder and stir into the sugar-nut mixture with the chopped walnuts. Spread the batter evenly in the pan and bake 50 minutes on the middle rack of the oven. Test with a toothpick. • Turn off the heat and leave the nut cake in the oven 10 minutes longer, then turn it out of the pan and cool. • Melt the chocolate in a double boiler. Pour over the cake and decorate with the reserved walnut halves.

## Ottilie Cake

**Easy to make**

Preparation time: 40 minutes
Baking time: 1 hour
Time to put the cake together:
15 minutes

Ingredients for a 12-inch loaf
pan

1 cup plus 1 tbs. butter

1¼ cups plus 1 tbs. sugar

½ tsp. vanilla

Pinch of salt

4 eggs

1 tbs. rum

1½ cups plus 1 tbs. flour

⅓ cup cornstarch

1 tsp. baking powder

4 oz. bittersweet chocolate

¾ cup  chopped almonds

¼ cup candied citron

⅔ cup bread crumbs

3 tbs. apricot jam

4 oz. chocolate

2 tbs. sliced almonds

Cream the butter. Stir in the sugar, vanilla, salt, eggs and rum a little at a time. Mix the flour with the cornstarch and baking powder and stir into the first mixture. • Preheat the oven to 350°. Butter the pan and sprinkle with the bread crumbs. • Coarsely grate the bittersweet chocolate and stir into the batter with the almonds and citron. • Spread the dough evenly in the pan and bake 1 hour on the middle rack of the oven. • Allow the cake to cool somewhat, then turn out onto a cake pan. • Rub the apricot jam through a sieve, heat it and brush it onto the cake. Melt the chocolate, pour over the cake and sprinkle the almond slices on the still warm glaze.

## Deer's Back Cake

**A famous recipe, easy to make**

Preparation time: 45 minutes
Baking time: 1 hour
Time to put the cake together:
15 minutes

Ingredients for 1 fluted "Deer's
Back" loaf pan

⅔ cup blanched almonds

1½ cups zwieback

7 tbs. softened butter

1 cup sugar

4 large or 5 medium eggs

2 tbs. flour

1½ tsp. baking powder

6½ oz. bittersweet chocolate

2 tbs. rum

⅔ cup bread crumbs

2½ tbs. coconut oil

⅓ cup slivered almonds

Grind the almonds in a nut grinder. Crush the zwieback between sheets of aluminum foil with a rolling pin, or grind them in the nut grinder. • Cream the butter. Slowly drizzle in the sugar. Add the eggs one at a time. Add the ground almonds, the crushed zwieback, flour and baking powder. Grate 2 ounces of the chocolate and add to the batter with the rum. • Preheat the oven to 350°. Butter the pan well and sprinkle with bread crumbs. Spread the batter in the pan and bake 1 hour on the middle rack of the oven. Test with a toothpick. Turn the cake out onto a cake rack and cool. • Melt the remaining chocolate with the coconut oil, pour over the cake and decorate with the almond slivers. Allow the glaze to harden.

## Countess Cake

**Somewhat difficult**

Preparation time: 1 hour
Baking time: 1 hour
Standing time: 1 day

Ingredients for a 12-inch loaf pan

⅔ cup bread crumbs
1 orange
1 cup plus 1 tbs. softened butter
1¼ cups plus 1 tbs. sugar
5 eggs
2 cups flour
½ cup plus 1 tbs. cornstarch
3 tsp. baking powder
6 tbs. apricot brandy or Cointreau
6½ oz. chocolate
4 oz. bittersweet chocolate glaze

Preheat the oven to 400°. Grease the pan well and sprinkle with bread crumbs. • Wash the orange in hot water, dry and grate the rind. Cream the butter. Add the sugar, orange rind and eggs a little at a time. Mix the flour with the cornstarch and baking powder. Stir into the first mixture 1 tablespoon at a time. • Spread the dough evenly in the pan and bake 1 hour on the lower rack of the oven. • Reverse the cake onto a cake rack and let stand 24 hours. • Squeeze the orange. Mix the juice with the brandy. • Cut the cake into 5 pieces slicing lengthwise from top to bottom. Soak in the liquid. • Melt the chocolate with the chocolate glaze in a bowl set in hot water and brush the glaze onto each slice. Carefully set the slices together and pour the glaze over the entire cake. Lay the cake on its side until the glaze has become quite firm.

## Tyrolean Chocolate Cake

**Easy to make, somewhat expensive**

Preparation time: 45 minutes
Baking time: 1 hour

Ingredients for a 12-inch loaf pan

1⅓ cups shelled almonds
5 oz. bittersweet chocolate
¾ cup plus 1 tbs. butter
1¼ cups plus 1 tbs. sugar
6 eggs
1 cup flour
1 tsp. baking powder
2 tbs. rum
⅔ cup bread crumbs
6½ oz. chocolate glaze

Grind the almonds in a nut grinder. Grate the chocolate. • Cream the butter, while slowly drizzling in the sugar. Separate the eggs. Add the yolks to the butter-sugar mixture one at a time. Combine the flour with the baking powder, sift it onto the first mixture, add the ground almonds and grated chocolate and mix. Beat the egg whites until stiff and fold into the batter with the rum. • Preheat the oven to 350°. Butter the pan and sprinkle with the bread crumbs. • Spread the batter evenly in the pan and bake 1 hour on the middle rack of the oven. Test with a toothpick. If the toothpick does not come out clean the cake needs to bake a few more minutes. Turn the heat off and leave the cake in the oven 10 minutes longer. • Turn the cake out onto a cake rack. Dissolve the chocolate glaze in a bowl set in hot water and pour it over the cake.

## Simple Butter Cake

### A Saxon specialty, easy to make

Preparation time: 45 minutes
Baking time: 30 minutes

Ingredients for 1 jelly roll pan

1¼ cups  low-fat ricotta
or cottage cheese

6 tbs. milk

7 tbs. oil

⅓ cup sugar

1 tsp. grated lemon rind

Pinch of salt

3 cups plus 1 tbs. flour

1 tbs. baking powder

¾ cup whipping cream

1¼ cups plus 1 tbs. sugar

2 tsp. cinnamon

7 tbs. butter

¾ cup plus 1 tbs. ground almonds

Preheat the oven to 400°. Butter the jelly roll pan. • Drain the cheese. In a bowl beat the cheese with the milk, oil, sugar, lemon rind and salt. Sift the flour with the baking powder over the cheese mixture, combine and knead together. • On a lightly floured surface roll out the dough to the size of the pan. With the back of a very large spoon press small indentations in the dough. Brush the dough with the cream. Mix the sugar with the cinnamon and sprinkle over the dough. Cut the butter into flakes over the indentations and sprinkle the almonds over the cake. • Bake the cake 30 minutes on the middle rack of the oven. • While it is still in the pan cut into 16 pieces and cool on a cake rack.

## Butter-Almond Cake

### Easy to make

Preparation time: 30 minutes
Baking time: 25 minutes

Ingredients for 1 jelly roll pan

¾ cup plus 1 tbs. whipping cream

⅔ cup sugar

2⅔ cups flour

1 tbs. baking powder

3 eggs

1 tsp. cinnamon

¾ cup plus 1 tbs. butter

1 cup sugar

6 tbs. whipping cream

1½ cups sliced almonds

Stir the cream with the sugar until the sugar is almost dissolved. Sift the flour with the baking powder over the sugar-cream mixture and stir in with a large spoon. Stir in the eggs, one at a time, with the cinnamon. • Preheat the oven to 350° and butter the pan. • Spread the dough evenly in the pan with a spatula. • Bake 10 minutes on the middle rack of the oven. • Melt the butter over low heat. Mix in the sugar, cream and sliced almonds and spread on the pre-baked dough. • Bake the cake 15 minutes longer, or until golden yellow. • Cut the cake into 16 pieces while it is still in the baking pan and cool on a cake rack.

# Cookie Cake

### Easy to make

Preparation time: 45 minutes
Chilling time: 4 hours

Ingredients for a 10-inch loaf pan

1 cup coconut oil

2 eggs

⅔ cup sugar

½ tsp. vanilla

½ cup instant cocoa

4 tbs. milk

⅓ heaping cup coarsely ground almonds

⅔ lb. butter cookies

**M**elt the coconut oil over low heat. Beat the eggs and add the sugar, vanilla, cocoa and milk. Add the lukewarm coconut oil and the almonds. • Line the pan with parchment paper, waxed paper or aluminum foil and cover with the chocolate mixture. Add a layer of cookies, more chocolate and so forth until all ingredients have been used. Place a plate on the cake to weight it down and chill 4 hours to make firm. • Turn the cookie cake out of the pan and remove the paper or foil. Cut into ½-inch slices. • Keep the cake in the refrigerator when not serving. It will stay fresh for at least a week.

Tip: Instead of making the cookie cake with butter cookies, use 9 zwieback. For adults use rum in the chocolate instead of milk, replace the sugar with powdered sugar and leave out the almonds.

# Birthday Tree

### Inexpensive and easy to make

Preparation time: 1 hour
Baking time: 12-15 minutes

3 eggs

Pinch of salt

⅔ cup sugar

½ tsp. vanilla

½ cup plus 1 tbs. flour

1 tsp. baking powder

⅓ cup plus 1 tbs. cornstarch

½ lb. (about 1 cup) strawberry jam

1 egg white

2 cups powdered sugar

Colored sugar

**P**reheat the oven to 350°. Separate the eggs. Beat the egg whites with the salt and ⅓ cup of the sugar. Beat the yolks with the remaining sugar and the vanilla. Mix the flour, baking powder and cornstarch and stir into the egg-sugar mixture with the egg whites. • Line a baking pan with parchment or waxed paper and butter the paper. Spread the batter evenly on the paper. • Bake the sponge cake 15 minutes or until golden brown, cool and remove the paper. • Meanwhile prepare the pattern for the tree. Cut a tree shape out of waxed paper and cut two trees from the cake. Spread one with well-stirred jam. Cut out small circles in the second with a tiny cookie cutter. Place the second tree on the first and fill the circles with more jam. • Beat the egg white with enough powdered sugar to make a thick, creamy liquid. Brush on the tree and decorate with colored sugar.

## Cheese Cake with Poppy Seeds

### Somewhat difficult

Preparation time: 1 hour
Baking time: 1¼ hours

Ingredients for an 11-inch springform pan

For the tart pastry:

2 cups flour

Generous pinch of baking powder

1 egg yolk

⅔ cup butter

⅓ cup sugar

½ tsp. vanilla

For the poppy seed filling:

⅓ heaping cup raisins

2 tbs. rum

1¾ scant cups ground poppy seeds

¾ cup sugar

Grated rind of ½ lemon

½ tsp. cinnamon

¼ cup softened butter

½ cup milk

For the cheese mixture:

2 cups ricotta or cottage cheese

¾ cup sugar

2 eggs

2 tbs. lemon juice

½ cup crème fraîche

2 heaping tbs. cornstarch

For the glaze:

1 egg yolk

Quickly knead the flour, baking powder, egg yolk, butter, sugar and vanilla into a smooth pastry dough and chill. • Wash the raisins in hot water, pat dry and soak in the rum. • Mix the poppy seeds with the sugar, lemon rind, cinnamon and butter. Heat the milk and pour over the poppy seed mixture. Set aside to soak. • Stir the cheese with the sugar. Separate the eggs and beat the egg whites until stiff. Stir the yolks, lemon juice, crème fraîche and cornstarch into the cheese mixture. Fold in the egg whites. • Preheat the oven to 350°. • Roll out the pastry dough to a thin sheet. Use it to line the buttered pan, shaping 1-inch sides. • Stir the raisins into the poppy seed mixture, spread over the pastry dough and cover with the cheese mixture. • Bake 75 minutes on the lower rack of the oven. • After 30 minutes whisk the egg yolk with 1 tablespoon of water and brush onto the cake.

## Cheese Cake without a Crust

### Easy to make

Preparation time: 20 minutes
Baking time: 1½ hours

Ingredients for an 11-inch springform pan

6 eggs

½ cup plus 1 tbs. butter

1½ cups sugar

3¼ cups ricotta or cottage cheese

2 cups cream cheese

1 package vanilla pudding mix

2 heaping tbs. cornstarch

⅔ cup  bread crumbs

Separate the eggs. • Cream the butter with the sugar, then add the egg yolks, one at a time. Stir in the briefly drained cheese, the cream cheese and pudding mix. Beat the egg whites until stiff and fold in with the cornstarch. • Preheat the oven to 350°. Butter the pan and sprinkle with the bread crumbs. Spread the cheese mixture evenly in the pan and bake 1 hour and 30 minutes or until golden brown.

## Cheese Cake with Streusel

**Easy to make**

Preparation time: 50 minutes
Baking time: 1 hour

Ingredients for an 11-inch springform pan:
For the streusel:
2 cups flour
¾ cup sugar
½ cup plus 1 tbs. butter
½ tsp. vanilla
1 egg yolk
Grated rind of ½ lemon
For the pan:
½ cup farina
For the cheese mixture:
4 cups ricotta or cottage cheese
½ cup plus 1 tbs. softened butter
1½ cups sugar
4 eggs
1 egg white
½ tsp. vanilla

Grated rind of 1 lemon
2 tbs. farina

**Q**uickly knead the flour with the sugar, butter, vanilla, egg yolk and lemon rind and crumble to make the streusel. • Preheat the oven to 400°. Butter the pan and sprinkle with farina. • Spread two-thirds of the streusel on the bottom of the pan and press lightly. Chill the remaining streusel. • Press some of the liquid from the cheese. Cream the butter with the sugar. Separate the eggs. Beat the egg yolks into the butter-sugar mixture. Beat the egg whites. Stir the vanilla, lemon rind, cheese and farina into the first mixture and fold in the egg whites. Pour the cheese mixture into the pan and spread evenly. Cover with the remaining streusel. • Bake the cake 1 hour.

## American Cheese Cake

**Easy to make, requires some time**

Preparation time: 45 minutes
Baking time: 1½ hours

Ingredients for a 10-inch springform pan
10 pieces zwieback
2 tbs. sugar
3½ tbs. butter
2½ cups cream cheese
¾ cup plus 1 tbs. sour cream
5 eggs
1 cup plus 1 tbs. sugar
Grated rind of ½ lemon
2 tbs. lemon juice
⅓ heaping cup cornstarch
1 tsp. baking powder

**P**lace the zwieback in plastic wrap and crush with a rolling pin. Add to the sugar and butter and knead to make a rich crumbly mixture. • Press the zwieback mixture evenly over the bottom of the pan. • Beat the cheese with the sour cream. Separate the eggs. Beat the yolks into the cheese mixture with the sugar, lemon rind and lemon juice. Beat the egg whites until stiff. Mix the cornstarch with the baking powder, sift over the cheese mixture and fold in with the egg whites. • Preheat the oven to 325°. Spread the cheese mixture evenly on the zwieback crust and bake 1½ hours on the lower rack of the oven, until golden brown. • Loosen the cake from the springform rim with a sharp knife and allow the cake to cool.

## Honey Cake

**Inexpensive and easy to make**

Preparation time: 30 minutes
Baking time: 1 hour

Ingredients for a 12-inch loaf pan

¾ cup plus 3 tbs. honey

¾ cup sugar

½ tsp. vanilla

1 egg

½ cup milk

½ tsp. cinnamon

Generous pinch of ground cloves

Generous pinch of ground cardamom

1 tsp. grated orange rind or dried lemon rind

2 cups whole-wheat flour

2 cups rye flour

1 tbs. baking powder

3 tbs. currant jam

3 tbs. cherry jam

3 tbs. elderberry jam

8 oz. chocolate glaze

**H**eat the honey with the sugar, vanilla, egg and milk, stirring constantly. Allow the mixture to cool, stirring occasionally, then add the spices, flour and baking powder. • Preheat the oven to 350°. Butter the pan. • Spread the dough in the pan and bake 1 hour, testing with a toothpick. Turn off the heat and leave the cake in the oven 10 minutes longer. • Stand the cooled cake on its side and slice into three long layers. Stir each jam until smooth, spread one kind of jam on each layer and stack the layers. • Pour the melted chocolate glaze over the cake. • It will develop the fullest aroma if allowed to stand a few days.

## Fruitcake

**A regional specialty**

Preparation time: 45 minutes
Baking time: 1 hour

Ingredients for a 10-inch loaf pan

½ cup candied citron

½ cup dried figs

¼ cup dried dates

⅓ cup currants

⅓ cup raisins

3 tbs. rum

1 cup hazelnuts

½ cup plus 1 tbs. butter

¾ cup sugar

5 eggs

¾ cup plus 1 tbs. flour

3 tsp. baking powder

1 cup chopped almonds

⅛ tsp cinnamon

Grated rind of ½ lemon

2 cups powdered sugar

3 tbs. lemon juice

¼ cup mixed candied fruit

**D**ice the citron, figs and pitted dates. Mix with the washed currants and raisins and sprinkle with the rum. Set aside to soak. • Grind the hazelnuts. • Cream the butter. Slowly add the sugar and the eggs one at a time. Mix the flour with the baking powder and fold into the first mixture. Mix the chopped almonds, ground hazelnuts and dried fruit into the batter with the cinnamon and lemon rind. • Preheat the oven to 350°. Line the pan with parchment or waxed paper. Spread the batter evenly in the pan and bake 1 hour. • Stir the powdered sugar and lemon juice, pour over the cake and decorate with candied fruit.

## Chocolate Pound Cake

### Inexpensive and easy to make

Preparation time: 20 minutes
Baking time: 1 hour

Ingredients for 1 bundt pan
⅔ cup bread crumbs
¾ cup softened butter
1¼ cups plus 1 tbs. sugar
½ tsp. vanilla
2 tbs. rum
Pinch of salt
5 eggs
2 cups flour
⅓ cup plus 1 tbs. cornstarch
2 tsp. baking powder
2 oz. powdered chocolate
2 tbs. apricot jam
6 oz. bittersweet chocolate

Preheat the oven to 350°. Butter the pan and sprinkle with the bread crumbs. • Cream the butter. Slowly mix in the sugar, vanilla, rum and salt and add the eggs one at a time. Mix the flour with the cornstarch, baking powder and powdered chocolate and stir into the batter 1 tablespoon at a time. • Spread the batter in the pan and bake 1 hour. • Heat the apricot jam. • Turn the cake out onto a rack, brush with the jam and allow to cool. • Melt the chocolate in a bowl set in hot water and pour it over the cake.

Tip: Those who prefer a cake with a fruity flavor can stir diced maraschino cherries into the batter.

## Gugelhupf

### A famous recipe

Preparation time: 50 minutes
Baking time: 1 hour

Ingredients for 1 large bundt pan
3¾ cups plus 1 tbs. flour
2 tsp. dry yeast
¾ cup sugar
½ cup lukewarm milk
1⅔ cups butter
5 eggs
Pinch of salt
Grated rind of 1 lemon
⅔ cup raisins
⅓ cup currants
½ cup chopped almonds
⅓ cup diced candied citron
2 tbs. powdered sugar

Place the flour in a bowl and make a well in the center. Add the yeast into the well and add 1 teaspoon of the sugar, half the milk and mix together with some of the flour. Cover and set aside 20 minutes to allow the sponge to form. • Melt the butter over low heat. Add the remaining milk and sugar, the eggs, salt and lemon rind. • Beat the butter mixture and the yeast sponge into the flour and knead together. Wash the raisins and currants in hot water, pat dry and add to the dough with the almonds and citron. • Place the yeast dough in the well greased pan, cover and allow to rise until it almost fills the pan. • Preheat the oven to 350°. Bake the Gugelhupf 1 hour on the lower rack of the oven. • Turn off the heat and leave the cake in the oven 10 minutes longer. • Turn the cake upside down, cover with a damp cloth and remove the pan after 10 minutes. • Sift powdered sugar over the cake.

## Poppy Seed-Walnut Streusel

**Nutritious**

Preparation time: 1¼ hours
Baking time: 30 minutes

Ingredients for an 11-inch loaf pan

For the dough:

1½ cups plus 1 tbs. whole-wheat flour

3 tbs. flour

¼ cup buckwheat flour

Grated rind of ½ lemon

1 tsp. dry yeast

⅔ cup honey

½ cup milk

For the filling:

1 cup whole walnuts

¾ cup plus 1 tbs. ground poppy seed

Generous pinch of cinnamon

4 tbs. milk

¼ cup butter

3 tbs. apricot jam

To make the dough mix the flours with the lemon rind, crumble the yeast into the center and mix with ⅓ of the honey, the milk and some of the flour. Cover and let stand 15 minutes. • Knead the rest of the flour into the yeast sponge and let rise 30 minutes. • Set aside a few walnuts for decoration and grind the rest. Mix with the poppy seed, cinnamon, remaining honey and milk and bring to a boil. Remove from the heat and mix in half the butter. Cool the mixture, stirring occasionally. • Roll out the dough to a 12 x 16-inch rectangle, spread with the filling and roll up beginning at the narrow end. Cut the roll in half lengthwise. • Preheat the oven to 400°. Butter the pan well. • Twist the pieces of dough around each other and lay in the pan, the dough side down. Melt the remaining butter and brush on the cake. Test with a toothpick. Turn off the heat and leave the cake in the oven 10 minutes longer, then spread with the marmalade and allow to cool in the pan.

## Cheese Stollen

**A famous recipe**

Preparation time: 30 minutes
Baking time: 1 hour

Ingredients for 1 stollen

¾ cup plus 1 tbs. cornstarch

3¾ cups plus 1 tbs. flour

1 tbs. baking powder

1¼ cups plus 1 tbs. sugar

3 eggs

1 cup low-fat ricotta or cottage cheese

1¼ cups raisins

½ tsp. vanilla

¼ cup finely diced candied citron

Grated rind of 1 lemon

¾ cup plus 1 tbs. butter

1 cup powdered sugar

1 tbs. rum

Mix the cornstarch with the flour, baking powder, sugar, eggs and drained cheese. Wash the raisins in hot water, pat dry and mix into the dough with the vanilla, citron and lemon rind. Cut the butter into pieces and knead in. • Preheat the oven to 400°. • Roll the dough into a rectangle with one thinner and one thicker side. Fold the thicker side over the thinner side. • Lay the stollen on a greased baking sheet and bake 1 hour or until golden brown. • Stir the powdered sugar with the rum and brush onto the cooled stollen.

## Almond Stollen

### A famous recipe

Preparation time: 50 minutes
Rising time: 1¾ hours
Baking time: 45 minutes

| Ingredients for 2 stollen loaves |
| --- |
| 2 tsp. dry yeast |
| ⅔ cup sugar |
| ¾ cup lukewarm milk |
| 3¾ cups plus 1 tbs. flour |
| 3 cups chopped almonds |
| 7 tbs. softened butter |
| 1 egg |
| Pinch of salt |
| 2 tbs. melted butter |
| ½ cup powdered sugar |

**M**ix the yeast with 1 teaspoon of the sugar and the milk. Set aside to form the sponge. • Mix half the flour with the almonds, butter, remaining sugar, egg, salt and yeast sponge. Add more flour if necessary. Knead well, cover and let rise 1 hour. • Shape 2 rectangles from the dough, rolling out one side thicker than the other, then fold the thicker over the thinner side. • Place the 2 stollen on a greased baking sheet, cover and let rise 30 minutes. • Preheat the oven to 425°. Place an oven-proof glass filled with water into the oven. • Bake the stollen 45 minutes. After 10 minutes remove the water and turn the heat down to 400°. After 45 minutes test with a toothpick. Turn off the heat and leave the stollen in the oven 10 minutes longer, then brush with the butter and sift a thick layer of powdered sugar over both cakes.

## Dresden Christmas Stollen

### A regional specialty

Preparation time: 40 minutes
Rising time: 1½ hours
Baking time: 1¼ hours

| Ingredients for 1 stollen |
| --- |
| 1¼ cups raisins |
| 1¼ cups currants |
| ½ cup candied orange rind |
| ½ cup candied citron |
| 1½ cups chopped almonds |
| 6 tbs. rum |
| 1 packet dry yeast |
| 5¾ cups flour |
| ⅔ cup sugar |
| 1 cup milk |
| 1 tsp. vanilla |
| 1¾ cups butter |
| Pinch of salt |
| 1 cup powdered sugar |

**W**ash the raisins and currants in hot water, dry and mix with the citron, orange rind and rum. Cover and allow to soak. • Add the yeast with the flour, stir with 1 tablespoon of the sugar, some of the milk and flour and set aside 30 minutes for the sponge to form. • Cut 1½ cups butter into shavings and sprinkle around the edges of the flour with the vanilla, sugar and salt. Knead into the flour with the yeast sponge and the remaining milk. Cover and let rise 30 minutes. • Quickly knead in the dried fruit. Roll out the dough, make an indentation down the middle and fold the long sides over each other. Lay on a well greased baking sheet and let rise 30 more minutes. • Preheat the oven to 400°. • Bake the stollen about 15 minutes on the lower rack of the oven, reduce the heat to 350° and bake 1 hour. • Brush the hot stollen with the remaining butter and cover with a heavy layer of sifted powdered sugar.

# Favorite
# Cookies
# and Pastries

## Jelly Roll with Lemon Cream

### Quick and easy to make

Preparation time: 15 minutes
Baking time: 10 minutes
Time to put the cake together:
15 minutes

| Ingredients for 1 jelly roll |
| --- |
| 4 egg whites |
| 1¼ cups plus 1 tbs. sugar |
| Pinch of salt |
| ½ tsp. vanilla |
| 8 egg yolks |
| ⅓ cup plus 1 tbs. flour |
| ⅓ cup plus 1 tbs. cornstarch |
| 2 cups whipping cream |
| 5 tbs. lemon juice |
| Grated rind of ½ lemon |
| 2 tbs. powdered sugar |

Preheat the oven to 400°. Line a jelly roll pan with parchment or waxed paper. Beat the egg whites until very stiff with ⅔ cup of the sugar, the salt and vanilla. Fold the egg yolks into the egg whites. Mix the flour with the cornstarch and mix in gently with the whisked egg mixture. • Spread the batter evenly in the pan and bake 10 minutes to a golden brown. • Turn the sponge cake out onto a kitchen towel sprinkled with 2 tablespoons of sugar and cover with a cold, damp towel. • Whip the cream until stiff with the lemon juice and rind, drizzling in the remaining sugar while whipping. • Remove the damp towel. Spread the lemon cream on the sponge cake. Roll up the cake with the aid of the towel underneath it. Cover with the powdered sugar.

## Jelly Roll with Raspberry Cream

### Quick and inexpensive

Preparation time: 15 minutes
Baking time: 8-10 minutes
Time to put the cake together:
15 minutes

| Ingredients for 1 jelly roll |
| --- |
| 4 eggs |
| Pinch of salt |
| 1 cup sugar |
| ½ tsp. vanilla |
| ½ cup plus 1 tbs. flour |
| ½ cup plus 1 tbs. cornstarch |
| 3 tbs. sugar |
| 1½ cups whipping cream |
| ½ lb. raspberries |

Preheat the oven to 425°. Line a jelly roll pan with parchment or waxed paper. • Separate the eggs and whip the whites until extremely stiff with the salt and half the sugar. • Beat the yolks with the remaining sugar and vanilla. Sift the flour and cornstarch over the yolk-sugar mixture and fold in with the egg whites. Spread evenly in the pan. • Bake the sponge cake 10 minutes on the upper rack of the oven to a golden brown. • Sprinkle a large damp kitchen towel with 2 tablespoons of sugar and turn the cake out onto the towel. Pull off the paper and roll up the cake with the aid of the towel. • Whip the cream and remaining sugar until stiff. Place half the cream in a pastry bag. Wash and dry the raspberries, setting aside a few for decoration. Mix the remaining berries with the whipped cream, roll out the cake and spread with the raspberry cream. Roll it up again and top with mounds of whipped cream, each with a raspberry in the center.

## Chocolate Roll with Cherries

**Easy to make**

Preparation time: 15 minutes
Baking time: 10 minutes
Time to put the cake together:
30 minutes
Chilling time: 30 minutes

4 eggs
¾ cup sugar
½ cup plus 1 tbs. flour
⅓ cup plus 1 tbs. cornstarch
1 cup powdered chocolate
½ tbs. gelatin
1 lb. sweet cherries
1⅓ cups cream cheese
2 tbs. lemon juice
¾ cup whipping cream
2 oz. bittersweet chocolate

Preheat the oven to 425°. Line a jelly roll pan with parchment or waxed paper. • Separate the eggs. Beat the yolks with 3 tablespoons of water and ⅓ cup plus 2 tablespoons sugar until lemon colored. Beat the egg whites until stiff. Fold into the yolk-sugar mixture with the flour, cornstarch and powdered chocolate. • Spread the batter evenly in the pan and bake 10 minutes. • Dissolve the gelatin in a little cold water. Wash, dry, pit and chop the cherries. Combine with the cream cheese and the remaining sugar. Heat the lemon juice. Stir in the dissolved gelatin and stir into the cherry-cheese mixture. • Turn the cake out onto a kitchen towel sprinkled with sugar. Pull off the paper and roll up the cake. • Whip the cream until stiff and mix 3 tablespoons whipped cream into the cherry-cheese mixture. Spread the sponge cake with the cream filling, roll it up and chill 1 hour. • Spread the chocolate roll with whipped cream. Grate the chocolate over the cake.

## Jelly Roll Slices with Peach Cream

**Easy to make**

Preparation time: 15 minutes
Baking time: 30 minutes
Time to put the cake together:
20 minutes
Chilling time: 1 hour

4 eggs
⅔ cup sugar
½ tsp. vanilla
¾ cup plus 1 tbs. flour
3½ tbs. cornstarch
1 lb. fully ripe peaches
¾ cup Cointreau
1 vanilla bean
2 tbs. sugar
¾ cup whipping cream

Preheat the oven to 425°. • Separate the eggs. Beat the yolks with 4 tablespoons of cold water, the sugar and vanilla until lemon colored. Beat the egg whites and fold into the yolk-sugar mixture with the flour and cornstarch. Spread the batter evenly in a jelly roll pan lined with parchment or waxed paper. • Bake the sponge cake 10 minutes, then turn out onto a damp cloth. • Prick the peaches well with a fork, dip in boiling water and remove the skins. Setting aside 1 peach for decoration, chop the remaining peaches very finely and sprinkle with the Cointreau. Add the soft center of the vanilla bean to the cream with the sugar. • Whip the cream until stiff and mix with the peach puree, setting aside ⅓ cup for decoration. Spread the sponge cake with the peach cream and roll up again. • Wrap the jelly roll in aluminum foil and chill 1 hour. Cut into 10 slices and decorate with mounds of whipped cream and slices of peach.

## Éclairs with Mocha Cream

**Easy to make, inexpensive**

Preparation time: 20 minutes
Baking time: 20-30 minutes
Time to put the cake together:
15 minutes

| Makes 12 |
|---|
| For the choux pastry: |
| 1 cup water |
| 3½ tbs. butter |
| 1 tbs. sugar |
| ½ tsp. vanilla |
| Pinch of salt |
| 1⅓ cups flour |
| 4 eggs |
| For the filling: |
| 1 cup whipping cream |
| 2 tsp. instant coffee |
| 1 tsp. sugar |
| For the glaze: |
| 1½ cups powdered sugar |

| |
|---|
| 1 tbs. instant coffee |
| 2 tbs. rum |

**P**reheat the oven to 425°. • In a saucepan bring the water to a boil with the butter, sugar, vanilla and salt. Remove from the heat. Add the flour all at once and stir vigorously. Place the pan over low heat and continue to stir until the dough comes away from the sides of the pan. Remove from the heat and stir in 1 egg. Cool the dough, stirring in the remaining eggs one at a time. • Place the dough in a pastry bag with a large flower tip and place about 12 finger-long strips of dough on a baking sheet, keeping them a good distance from one another. Bake the éclairs 20 to 30 minutes on the middle rack of the oven. • To make the filling whip the cream with the coffee and sugar and place in a pastry tube.

• Cut the éclairs in half immediately and allow to cool. • To make the glaze stir the powdered sugar with 1 tablespoon hot water, the coffee and rum. Brush the glaze onto the tops of the éclairs. Pipe the cream onto the bottoms and cover with the lids.

## Small Cream Puffs

**Quick and easy to make**

Preparation time: 30 minutes
Baking time: 20 minutes

| Makes 40 cream puffs |
|---|
| ½ cup water |
| 3½ tbs. butter |
| Pinch of salt |
| 2 tbs. sugar |
| 1 tsp. vanilla |
| 1 cup flour |
| 4 eggs |

| |
|---|
| 1½ cups whipping cream |
| 1 tbs. powdered sugar |

**I**n a saucepan bring the water to a boil with the butter, salt, sugar and ½ teaspoon of the vanilla. Add the flour all at once and stir until the dough comes away from the sides of the pan. • Place the choux paste in a bowl and allow to cool somewhat. Add the eggs one at a time. • Preheat the oven to 425°. Grease a baking sheet. • Place the dough in a pastry bag with a flower tip and place walnut-sized mounds on the baking sheet. • Bake the cream puffs about 20 minutes to a golden brown. • To make the filling whip the cream with the remaining vanilla, and powdered sugar. Place in a pastry tube. Cut the puffs in half and fill with the cream. Sprinkle with powdered sugar and allow to cool.

## Currant Rolls

### A regional specialty

Preparation time: 20 minutes
Rising time: 1 hour
Baking time: 20 minutes

| |
| --- |
| Makes 12 rolls |
| 3¾ cups plus 1 tbs. flour |
| 2 tsp. dry yeast |
| ⅓ cup sugar |
| Pinch of salt |
| Pinch of cinnamon |
| Pinch of ground cardamom |
| 1 tsp. grated lemon rind |
| 1 cup lukewarm milk |
| 7 tbs. softened butter |
| 1 egg |
| ½ cup currants |
| 2 cups whipping cream |
| 2 tbs. powdered sugar |

**M**ix the flour with the yeast, sugar, salt, cinnamon, cardamom and lemon rind. Add the milk, butter and egg. Knead the dough well for 5 minutes. Wash the currants in hot water, dry and add to the dough. Sprinkle the dough with some flour, cover and set in a warm place 45 minutes to rise. • Quickly knead the dough with floured hands; roll into a long strip. Cut into 12 equal pieces and shape them into rolls. • Place on a greased baking sheet. Cover and let rise 15 minutes. • Preheat the oven to 400°. • Brush the rolls with a little milk and bake on the middle rack of the oven for 20 minutes or until golden brown. • Cool the rolls on a cake rack, then cut but not all the way through. • Whip the cream until stiff, place in a pastry bag with a flower tip and fill the rolls with cream. Cover with powdered sugar.

## Nut Crescents

### A Danish specialty

Preparation time: 30 minutes
Rising time: 1¼ hours
Baking time: 20-25 minutes

| Makes 12 |
| --- |
| 1½ tsp. dry yeast |
| 1 tsp. sugar |
| ½ cup lukewarm milk |
| 2⅓ cups flour |
| Pinch of salt |
| 1 egg |
| 1 tbs. butter |
| ¾ cup plus 1 tbs. ground hazelnuts |
| ⅓ cup brown sugar |
| Pinch of cinnamon |
| 3 tbs. evaporated milk |
| 1 cup powdered sugar |
| 2 tbs. rum |

Stir the yeast with the sugar and some warm milk and set aside 15 minutes to form the sponge. • Place half the flour in a bowl. Add the remaining milk, the yeast sponge, salt and egg. Knead to a smooth dough, and then knead in the remaining flour. Cover and let rise 45 minutes. • Melt the butter, add the hazelnuts and sauté briefly. Mix in the sugar, cinnamon and evaporated milk. • Knead the dough thoroughly. On a lightly floured surface roll out into a rectangle. Cut out long triangles. Spread the centers with hazelnut mixture. Roll them up toward the pointed end and bend into crescents. Place on a greased baking sheet and let rise 15 minutes more. • Preheat the oven to 400°. • Bake the crescents to a golden brown, 20-25 minutes. • Stir the powdered sugar with the rum and brush it onto the crescents.

## Nut Combs

### Easy to make

Thawing time: 1 hour
Preparation time: 30 minutes
Baking time: 15-20 minutes

| Makes 10 nut combs |
| --- |
| ⅔ lb. frozen puff pastry |
| 1 cup ground hazelnuts |
| 1 tbs. butter |
| 1 egg |
| ⅔ cup sugar |

Thaw the pieces of frozen pastry next to one another. • Cut the pastry into 10 pieces and roll out on a floured surface to 4-inch squares. • Sauté the ground nuts lightly in the butter and allow to cool. Separate the egg. Beat the egg white and fold in the sugar and nuts. • Preheat the oven to 425°. • Beat the egg yolk with 1 tablespoon water. • Spread some of the hazelnut mixture on each of the pastry squares, leaving wide margins. Brush the edges with the egg yolk and fold the squares together. • Lay the nut combs on a baking sheet just rinsed with cold water, bending them out a little. Brush them with the remaining egg yolk and bake 15-20 minutes on the middle rack of the oven.

# Elephants' Ears

**A famous recipe, easy to make**

Thawing time: 1 hour
Preparation time: 20 minutes
Chilling time: 30 minutes
Baking time: 16-20 minutes

Makes 30 elephants' ears

⅔ lb. frozen puff pastry

⅔ cup sugar

Thaw the pieces of puff pastry next to each other on a sugared work surface. • To roll them, sugar the surface again and roll out to an 8 x 12-inch rectangle. Turn the dough frequently while rolling out. Fold the long sides of the dough into the middle without letting them touch and sprinkle with some sugar. Cover and chill 30 min-

utes. • Preheat the oven to 425°. Rinse a baking sheet with cold water. • With a sharp knife cut pencil-thick slices from the pastry roll. Lay them on the baking sheet spacing them well and bake 8 to 10 minutes, turn them and bake 8 to 10 minutes longer. • Cool the elephants' ears on another baking sheet.

Tip: Elephants' ears are especially good topped with raspberries and mounds of whipped cream. Sugared currants or slices of mango can also be used for a change. All by themselves elephants' ears are a classic pastry to have with tea.

# Tea Leaves

**Easy to make, a regional specialty**

Thawing time: 1 hour
Preparation time: 30 minutes
Chilling time: 15 minutes
Baking time: 16 minutes

Makes 16 tea leaves

⅔ lb. frozen puff pastry

⅔ cup sugar

2 oz. chocolate

Thaw the pieces of frozen pastry next to each other, then roll them out on a sugared work surface to a rectangle about ¼ inch thick. • Cut out 4 to 5-inch circles with a cookie cutter or glass, and lay them on a sugared work surface. With a rolling pin roll them in one direction, turn and roll again in the same

direction. Lay the ovals on a baking sheet rinsed with cold water and chill 15 minutes. • Preheat the oven to 425°. • Bake the "tea leaves" 8 minutes on the middle rack of the oven, turn them over and bake 8 minutes longer. • Transfer the pastries to another baking sheet to cool. • Melt the chocolate in a bowl set in hot water and dip the end of each pastry in the chocolate. Set on a cake rack until the chocolate is dry.

Tip: Tea leaves can be garnished with whipped cream flavored with a few tablespoons of brandy. Pour a thin stream of chocolate sauce over the whipped cream. In this variation there is no need to dip the pastries in chocolate.

## Copenhagen Snails

### A Danish specialty

Preparation time: 2 hours
Baking time: 12-15 minutes

Makes 20 snails

For the yeast dough:

3¾ cups plus 1 tbs. flour

2 tsp. dry yeast

⅓ cup plus 2 tbs. sugar

1 cup milk

2 egg yolks

⅓ cup butter

Pinch of salt

Pinch of cardamom

For the butter dough:

⅔ cup flour

1 cup plus 1 tbs. chilled butter

For the filling:

⅔ cup currants

2½ oz. almond paste

¾ cup powdered sugar

1 egg white

1 tsp. cinnamon

2 tbs. sugar

For the glaze:

1 egg white

**P**lace the flour in a bowl. In a well in the flour stir the yeast with 1 teaspoon of the sugar and a little of the milk. Set aside 15 minutes to form the sponge. • For the butter dough quickly knead the flour with the butter, roll out between sheets of waxed paper to a rectangle about ½ inch thick and chill. • Knead into the yeast sponge all the remaining yeast dough ingredients. Let rise 30 minutes, then roll out to a rectangle twice the size of the butter dough. Lay the butter dough in the center and fold the yeast dough over. Roll out, fold over twice to make 3 layers and chill 15 minutes. Repeat the process twice. • Soak the currants. Mix the almond paste with the powdered sugar and egg white. Mix the cinnamon with the sugar.

• Roll out the dough to a 16 x 22-inch sheet. Cover with the almond paste, currants and cinnamon sugar. Roll up from the long sides toward the middle and cut slices 1 inch thick. • Preheat the oven to 425°. • Brush the snails with the beaten egg white and bake 12 to 15 minutes.

## Windmills

### Nutritious whole-wheat recipe

Preparation time: 1½ hours
Chilling time: about 12 hours
Baking time: 20-25 minutes

Makes 18 windmills

3¾ cups plus 1 tbs. whole-wheat flour

2 tsp. dry yeast

1 tbs. honey

1 cup milk

1 egg yolk

¾ cup plus 1 tbs. butter

1¼ cups ground almonds

⅔ cup rose hip butter

**M**ake a well in 3½ cups of the flour and crumble the yeast in the center. Stir with the honey, milk and some of the flour. Cover and set aside 15 minutes to form the sponge. • Add the egg yolk and 1 tablespoon of the butter, knead together, cover and chill 12 hours. • Mix the remaining flour and chilled butter and roll out to an 8 x 8-inch rectangle. • Roll out the dough to an 18 x 18-inch rectangle and place the butter-flour rectangle on one half of the dough. Fold over and press the edges together. Roll out the dough four times to full size, folding it over and chilling after each "turn." • Preheat the oven to 400°. • Roll out the dough and cut out 5-inch squares. Mix the almonds and rose hip butter and place a mound of the mixture in the center of each square. Cut straight in from the sides of the squares and fold four tips toward the center to form windmills. Bake 20 to 25 minutes on a greased baking sheet to a golden brown.

## Raisin Snails

### Easy to make

Preparation time: 40 minutes
Chilling time: 1 hour
Baking time: 25-30 minutes

Makes 20 snails

| |
|---|
| 1 cup low-fat ricotta or cottage cheese |
| 1 cup plus 2 tbs. chilled butter |
| Pinch of salt |
| ¼ tsp. vanilla |
| 2 cups flour |
| 1 tsp. baking powder |
| ¾ cup raisins |
| ⅓ cup ground hazelnuts |
| 1 tsp. cinnamon |
| ⅓ cup sugar |
| 1½ cups powdered sugar |
| 1-2 tbs. lemon juice |

**D**rain the cheese in a sieve. Cut 1 cup plus 1 tablespoon of the butter into flakes and add to the cheese with the salt, vanilla, flour and baking powder. Knead in a mixer with the dough hook, then knead by hand on a floured surface to a smooth dough. Wrap in aluminum foil and chill 1 hour. • On a floured surface roll out to a 16 x 24-inch rectangle. Melt the remaining butter in a saucepan; allow to cool somewhat. Brush on the dough. Wash the raisins in hot water, dry and mix with the ground nuts, cinnamon and sugar. Spread on the dough. • Roll up the dough starting with the narrow side. With a knife dipped in cold water cut into 20 pieces. • Preheat the oven to 400°. Grease a baking sheet. • Place the snails on the baking sheet and bake 20 to 30 minutes on the middle rack of the oven until golden brown. • Mix the powdered sugar with the lemon juice to a smooth, thick consis-

tency and brush on the snails while still warm. Cool the pastries on a cake rack.

## Chocolate-Covered Cup Cakes

### A famous recipe

Preparation time: 30 minutes
Baking time: 15 minutes

| Makes 16 |
| --- |
| 4 eggs |
| Pinch of salt |
| 1¼ cups plus 1 tbs. sugar |
| 1 tsp. vanilla |
| ½ cup plus 1 tbs. flour |
| ¾ cup plus 1 tbs. cornstarch |
| 1 tsp. baking powder |
| 2 tsp. gelatin |
| 2-3 plums pickled with ginger |
| ¾ cup whipping cream |
| Grated rind of ½ lemon |
| 4 oz. bittersweet chocolate |
| Grated rind of 1 orange |

Separate the eggs. Beat the egg whites and salt until stiff. Beat the yolks with 3 to 4 tablespoons hot water until lemon colored, then drizzle in the sugar and vanilla while continuing to beat. Gently fold the egg whites, the flour, cornstarch and baking powder into the yolk-sugar mixture. • Preheat the oven to 400°. • Set the paper cups on a baking sheet or in a cup cake pan and fill each with 2 to 3 tablespoons of batter. • Bake 15 minutes, then allow to cool. • For the filling dissolve the gelatin in a little cold water. Chop the ginger plums. Whip the cream until stiff and fold in the plums and lemon rind. Briefly warm the gelatin over low heat and fold into the cream. • Cut the cup cakes across the middle and fill with the ginger cream. • Melt the chocolate in a bowl set in hot water and pour over the cup cakes. • Sprinkle the grated or-

ange rind over the slightly liquid chocolate coating.

## Americans

### Nutritious whole-wheat recipe, easy to make

Preparation time: 30 minutes
Baking time: 15-20 minutes

| Makes 12 |
| --- |
| 1½ cups plus 1 tbs. whole-wheat flour |
| ¾ cup plus 1 tbs. corn flour |
| 3½ tbs. cornstarch |
| ½ tsp. vanilla |
| 1 cup plus 1 tbs. softened butter |
| ⅓ cup plus 2 tbs. honey |
| ¾ cup whipping cream |
| 1 egg |
| ¾ cup spreadable clover or honey |
| 2 drops natural lemon extract |

Mix the flour with the corn flour and cornstarch. • Mix ⅔ cup of the butter with the honey and vanilla. Stir in the dry ingredients alternately with the cream and the egg. Stir well and set aside 15 minutes. • Grease a baking sheet. Preheat the oven to 400°. • Using a large spoon place 12 mounds of batter on the baking sheet, spacing well. Bake 15 to 20 minutes to a golden brown, then allow to cool. • Cream the remaining butter. Gradually add the clover or honey and lemon extract. Spread the flat sides of the cookies with the honey glaze. • These cookies keep fresh for about four days and taste best one day after baking.

## Apple Turnovers

**Requires some time**

Preparation time: 1½ hours
Baking time: 20 minutes

Makes 15 turnovers

For the dough:

⅔ cup ricotta or cottage cheese

6 tbs. oil

5 tbs. milk

⅓ cup sugar

1 tsp. vanilla

2⅓ cups flour

2 tsp. baking powder

For the filling:

⅓ cup raisins

1 tbs. rum

1 lb. tart apples

2 tbs. lemon juice

⅓ cup plus 2 tbs. sugar

½ tsp. cinnamon

For the glaze:

1 cup powdered sugar

1-2 tbs. apple brandy or lemon juice

**D**rain or press the liquid out of the cheese. • For the filling wash the raisins in hot water, pat dry and sprinkle with rum. Quarter, peel and core the apples. Dice and mix with the lemon juice, sugar and cinnamon. Combine with the raisins and cook 10 minutes over low heat. • Beat the cheese with the oil, milk, sugar and vanilla. Mix the flour with the baking powder and fold into the cheese mixture 1 tablespoon at a time; knead together. • Roll the dough out to a fairly thick consistency and cut out 4-inch circles. Place a small mound of the cooled apple filling in the center of each circle, fold over and press the edges together with a fork. • Preheat the oven to 400°. • Place the turnovers on a greased baking sheet and bake 20 minutes to a golden brown. For the glaze, combine the powdered sugar with the apple brandy and brush over the turnovers.

## Sweet Pretzels

**Somewhat difficult, quick to make**

Preparation time: 20 minutes
Chilling time: 30 minutes
Baking time: 25-30 minutes

Makes 30 pretzels

3¾ cups plus 1 tbs. flour

2 tsp. baking powder

2 tsp. sugar

Generous pinch of salt

½ tsp. vanilla

½ cup sour cream

1 cup plus 2 tbs. chilled butter

1 egg white

⅔ cup sugar crystals

**S**ift the flour with the baking powder onto a work surface. Sprinkle the sugar and salt over the flour, make a well and pour in the sour cream and vanilla. Cut the butter into flakes around the rim of flour and chop all the ingredients with a broad knife, then quickly knead into a smooth dough. • Cover and chill 30 minutes. • Divide into 4 portions. On a lightly floured work surface roll out each portion to a 12-inch square about ⅛ inch thick. Cut out ½-inch strips and carefully twist them. • Preheat the oven to 425°. Line a baking sheet with parchment or waxed paper. • Shape the pastry twists into pretzels on the paper. • Lightly beat the egg white and brush onto the pretzels. Sprinkle with the sugar crystals and bake 25 to 30 minutes to a golden brown.

## Coconut Cup Cakes

### Nutritious, easy to make

Preparation time: 30 minutes
Baking time: 15-20 minutes

Makes 20

1⅓ cups coconut oil

1½ cups grated coconut

1½ cups plus 1 tbs. whole-wheat flour

⅓ cup plus 1 tbs. buckwheat flour

3½ tbs. cornstarch

2 tsp. baking powder

Grated rind of ½ lemon

3 drops natural lemon extract

¼ cup diced candied citron

¼ cup diced candied orange rind

¾ cup honey

4 eggs

6 tbs. coconut liqueur

**M**elt the coconut oil and cool. Toast the grated co-conut in a dry pan to a pale gold color. • Mix the flour with the cornstarch, baking powder, lemon rind, lemon extract and candied fruit. • Beat the coconut oil with the honey until foamy. Stir in the flour mixture alternately with the eggs and 1¼ cups of the grated coconut. • Preheat the oven to 350°. Set the paper cups on a baking sheet or cup cake pan and fill ¾ full with the batter. Sprinkle with the remaining coconut and bake 15 to 20 minutes to a golden brown. • Sprinkle each cup cake with 1 teaspoon coconut liqueur, cool and serve on a cooled platter.

## Coconut Crisps

### Nutritious

Preparation time: 1¼ hours
Baking time: 15 minutes

Makes 20 cookies

3 cups plus 1 tbs. whole-wheat flour

2 tsp. baking powder

Grated rind of ½ lemon

¾ cup plus 1 tbs. butter

⅓ cup plus 1 tbs. honey

4 eggs

¾ cup plus 1 tbs. currant jelly

3 cups grated coconut

⅓ cup plus 2 tbs. unrefined granulated sugar

For the glaze:

4 tbs. milk

**F**or the dough mix the flour with the baking powder and lemon rind. Make a well in the middle, cut the butter into flakes and sprinkle into the well with the honey and 1 egg. Knead well. Set aside 10 minutes. • Roll out two-thirds of the dough to a rectangle ¼ inch thick. Lay it on a greased baking sheet and spread with the jelly. Roll out the remaining dough, cut into strips about 1½-inches wide. Set them on the jelly about 1-inch apart. Brush with the milk. • Preheat the oven to 400°. • Toast the coconut in a dry pan stirring constantly until pale gold. Allow to cool slightly and stir with the sugar and remaining 3 eggs. Spread the coconut mixture on the jelly. • Bake 15 minutes or until golden brown. • Cut down the middle of the strips of dough and diagonally across the cake to make pieces about 2⅕-inches wide.

## Nut-Nougat Triangles

### Quick and easy to make

Preparation time: 30 minutes
Baking time: 20 minutes
Time to put the cake together: 15 minutes

Makes 20

| ⅔ cup softened butter |
|---|
| 1 cup sugar |
| ½ tsp. vanilla |
| 3 eggs |
| 1¼ cups flour |
| ½ cup plus 1 tbs. cornstarch |
| 1 tsp. baking powder |
| ½ cup cocoa |
| ¾ cups ground hazelnuts |
| 4 tbs. milk |
| 20 whole hazelnuts |
| 4 oz. nougat |
| 4 oz. chocolate |

**P**reheat the oven to 400°. Line a jelly roll pan with parchment or waxed paper. • Cream the butter with the sugar and vanilla, then add the eggs one at a time. Mix the flour with the cornstarch, baking powder, cocoa and ground nuts and stir into the first mixture alternately with the milk. • Spread the batter in the pan and bake 20 minutes on the middle rack of the oven. • Toast the nuts in a dry pan and remove the skins. Warm the nougat until it is spreadable. Melt the chocolate in a bowl set in hot water. • Cut the cake into squares, spread nougat on half the squares and top with the remaining squares. • Cut the squares diagonally and pour the melted chocolate over them. Press the skinned hazelnuts into the warm chocolate.

## Oatmeal Cookies

**Easy to make, inexpensive**

Preparation time: 1 hour
Baking time: 20 minutes

Makes 20 cookies

| ⅔ cup butter |
|---|
| 3¾ cups oat flakes |
| 2 cups plus 1 tbs. sugar |
| 2⅓ cups flour |
| 2 tsp. baking powder |
| ⅓ cup plus 1 tbs. ground almonds |
| 3 tsp. cocoa |
| 1 egg |
| 1 egg yolk |
| ⅓ cup sugar-beet syrup |
| ⅔ cup whole-oat flakes |
| 3 egg whites |
| Pinch of salt |
| ½ tsp. vanilla |
| 1 cup raisins |

**C**ut all but 1 tablespoon of the butter into flakes and mix with 2¼ cups of the oat flakes, 1¼ cups plus 1 tbs. of the sugar, the flour, baking powder, almonds, cocoa, egg, egg yolk and syrup. • Toast the whole-oat flakes in the remaining tablespoon of butter until light brown. Beat the egg whites with the salt until stiff. Drizzle in the remaining sugar and add the vanilla while whipping. • Wash the raisins in hot water, dry and mix with the toasted whole-oat flakes and the remaining oat flakes. • Preheat the oven to 350°. Lightly butter a baking sheet. On a floured surface roll out the dough ¼ inch thick and cut out 40 2½-inch circles. • Place a mound of filling on each of 20 circles, top with the remaining circles and press lightly together. Bake about 20 minutes on the middle rack of the oven. • These oatmeal cookies can be kept fresh in a closed container for 1 or 2 weeks.

## Walnut Cup Cakes

**Nutritious whole-wheat recipe**

Preparation time: 25 minutes
Baking time: 15-20 minutes

Makes 20

1¼ cups whole walnuts

¾ cup plus 1 tbs. rye flour

¾ cup plus 1 tbs. whole-wheat flour

2 tsp. baking powder

5 tsp. cocoa

½ tsp. vanilla

Grated rind of 1 orange

⅔ cup softened butter

⅔ cup honey

¼ cup molasses

3 eggs

Grind ⅔ of the nuts and chop the rest. Mix the flour with the baking powder, 4 teaspoons of the cocoa, ½ the grated orange rind and the ground nuts. • Cream the butter with ½ cup plus 1 tablespoon of the honey, the molasses and ¼ teaspoon of the vanilla. Stir in the dry ingredients alternately with the eggs. Beat thoroughly. • Preheat the oven to 350°. • Set the paper cups on a baking sheet or cup cake pan and fill ¾ full with the batter. Mix the chopped nuts with the remaining cocoa, vanilla, honey and orange rind. • Place a spoonful of filling in the center of each cup cake and press in lightly. • Bake the cup cakes 15 to 20 minutes. • They taste best the next day and stay fresh at least 5 days.

## Almond-Meringue Tartlets

**Requires some time**

Preparation time: 30 minutes
Drying time: 2 hours

Makes 12

4 egg whites

2 cups powdered sugar

1 tsp. lemon juice

⅓ cup plus 1 tbs. finely ground almonds

1 lb. mixed fruits in season

1 ¼-oz. package gelatin

2 tbs. sugar

1 cup apple juice

Whip the egg whites until stiff, gradually add the powdered sugar and lemon juice. Place the bowl in hot water and continue beating the egg whites until they are very stiff. This takes about 15 min-utes. • Fold the almonds into the egg whites. • Preheat the oven to 200°. Line a baking sheet with parchment or waxed paper. • Place the meringue in a pastry bag with a flower tip and pipe 12 flat 3-inch circles onto the paper, moving in a spiral from the center. Set "kisses" (small mounds) of meringue around the edges. Dry the meringues in the oven for about 2 hours, propping the oven door open a crack with the handle of a wooden spoon. • Remove the meringues from the paper. Wash or peel the fruit, remove the pits if necessary, slice and spread in the meringues. Add the gelatin with the sugar, and a little of the apple juice and stir well, then add the remaining apple juice and bring to a boil. Remove from the heat. • Pour the glaze over the fruit.

# Rose-Marzipan Cookies

## Nutritious whole-wheat recipe

Preparation time: 50 minutes
Baking time: 20-30 minutes

Makes 20 cookies

| |
|---|
| 1½ cups blanched almonds |
| ¾ cup plus 3 tbs. honey |
| 3 tbs. rose water |
| 3 eggs |
| ½ cup rose hip butter |
| 3 cups plus 1 tbs. whole-wheat flour |
| 2 tsp. baking powder |
| ½ tsp. cinnamon |
| ½ tsp. vanilla |
| ¾ cup chilled butter |

To make the marzipan grind 1 cup of the almonds in a food processor until very fine and mix with ¼ cup plus 1 tablespoon of the honey to a smooth consistency, placing the bowl in a saucepan of hot water. • Add 2 tablespoons of the rose water and rose hip butter. • Separate the eggs. Cut the butter into flakes and quickly mix with the flour, baking powder, cinnamon, vanilla, egg yolks and ⅓ cup of the honey to form a smooth pastry dough. On a floured surface roll out ¼-inch thick and cut out 3-inch circles with a cookie cutter or a glass. • Preheat the oven to 325°. Grease a baking sheet. • Lay the circles of pastry on the baking sheet and spread with the marzipan. • Grind the remaining almonds in an almond grinder. Beat the egg whites until stiff and mix with the remaining honey, rose water and ground almonds. Spread the mixture on the cookies and bake 20 to 30 minutes. • These cookies taste best 1 or 2 days after baking.

# Filled Millet Cakes

## Nutritious

Preparation time: 45 minutes
Baking time: 10-15 minutes

Makes 8

| |
|---|
| ½ cup milk |
| 3½ tbs. butter |
| ¼ tsp. vanilla |
| ⅔ cup millet flour |
| ⅓ cup plus 1 tbs. honey |
| 5 eggs |
| 2 tbs. cornstarch |
| ½ cup sugar-free strawberry jam |
| 1 cup whipping cream |
| 1 oz. chocolate |

Bring the milk to a boil with the butter and vanilla. Gradually stir in the millet flour. As soon as the batter is thoroughly thickened remove from the heat and stir in the honey. • Separate the eggs. Stir in the egg yolks alternately with the cornstarch. Beat the egg whites until stiff and fold into the batter. • Preheat the oven to 400°. Line a baking sheet with parchment or waxed paper. • Spread the batter on the baking sheet and bake 15 minutes to a golden brown. • Cut the cake into 16 pieces while still hot. When cool spread 8 pieces with the jam. Whip the cream until stiff and spread or press from a pastry bag onto the jam, then top with the remaining pieces of cake. • Melt the chocolate in a bowl set in hot water and dribble over the millet cakes.

## Jelly Doughnuts

**A festive specialty, inexpensive**

Preparation time: 40 minutes
Rising time: 1¼ hours
Frying time: about 30 minutes

| | |
|---|---|
| Makes 12 doughnuts | |
| 2 tsp. dry yeast | |
| ½ cup lukewarm milk | |
| ⅔ cup sugar | |
| 3¾ cups plus 1 tbs. flour | |
| Pinch of salt | |
| Grated rind of 1 lemon | |
| 2 eggs | |
| ⅓ cup softened butter | |
| ½ cup apricot, plum or raspberry jam | |
| For frying: | |
| 2 lbs. (6⅔ cups) oil | |
| For sifting: | |
| 2 tbs. powdered sugar | |

**P**our the yeast in a bowl, stir with the milk and 1 teaspoon of the sugar. Set aside about 15 minutes for the sponge to form. • Mix half the flour, the remaining sugar, salt, lemon rind and eggs with the yeast sponge, then add the butter and the remaining flour. Knead thoroughly until the dough comes away from the sides of the bowl. Cover and let rise 45 minutes. • Knead thoroughly one more time. On a floured surface roll out the dough ½ inch thick. Cut out 24, 3-inch circles with a cookie cutter or a glass. Place 1 teaspoon of jam in the center of 12 circles, brush the edges with water, cover with the other circles and press the edges together. • Heat the oil to 350°. Fry the doughnuts a few at a time on both sides for about 4 to 5 minutes or until golden brown. Drain and cover with powdered sugar.

Tip: Bavarian Doughnuts are made with the same dough. Pull the circles apart with buttered fingers to make the centers very thin and the rims thick. Fry them on both sides for about 3 to 4 minutes or until golden brown.

## Fresh Cheese Doughnuts

**Easy to make, inexpensive**

Preparation time: 20 minutes
Frying time: about 30 minutes

| | |
|---|---|
| Makes 20 doughnuts | |
| ⅓ cup softened butter | |
| 1 tsp. grated lemon rind | |
| Pinch of salt | |
| ⅓ cup sugar | |
| 1 egg | |
| ½ cup low-fat ricotta or cottage cheese | |
| 2 cups flour | |
| 1 tsp. baking powder | |
| 2-3 tbs. milk | |
| ¾ cup raisins | |
| For frying: | |
| 2 lbs. (6⅔ cups) oil | |
| For sifting: | |
| 3 tbs. powdered sugar | |

**H**eat the oil in the deep fryer to 350°. • Beat the butter with 1 teaspoon lemon rind, salt, sugar, egg and drained cheese. Mix the flour with the baking powder and add to the first mixture alternately with the milk and the washed raisins. • Fry 4 or 5 doughnuts at a time on all sides for about 3 to 4 minutes, or until golden brown. Sift powdered sugar over the doughnuts.

# Pastry-Bag Doughnuts

**A famous recipe, somewhat difficult**

Preparation time: 20 minutes
Standing time: 30 minutes
Frying time: about 30 minutes

| |
| --- |
| Makes 10 doughnuts |
| 1 cup water |
| 3½ tbs. butter |
| Pinch of salt |
| 1 cup flour |
| 3 eggs |
| For the glaze: |
| 2 cups powdered sugar |
| 2 tbs. rum or lemon juice |
| For frying: |
| 2 lbs. (6⅔ cups) oil |

Bring the water to a boil in a saucepan with the butter and salt. Add the flour all at once and stir until the dough comes away from the pan. Remove from the heat and cool somewhat. Mix in the eggs one at a time. The dough should be shiny and hang from the spoon in long pointed drips. • Let the dough stand at room temperature for 30 minutes. • Heat the oil to 350°. Pull four 3-inch strips of waxed paper through the hot oil. • Place the dough in a pastry bag with a large flower tip and pipe a wreath about ½-inch high onto each strip of paper. Turn the wreaths upside down into the oil, remove the paper when the pastries have slid off. Cook all the doughnuts in this way, frying on both sides to a golden brown in about 4 minutes. Remove from the oil with a slotted spoon and drain on absorbent paper. • Mix the powdered sugar with 2 tablespoons of hot water and whisk with the rum or lemon juice. Dip one side of the doughnuts in the glaze and cool on a cake rack.

## Skirt Cakes

**Inexpensive, requires some time**

Preparation time: 40 minutes
Standing time: 30 minutes
Frying time: about 45 minutes

| |
| --- |
| Makes 30 doughnuts |
| 7 tbs. softened butter |
| ⅔ cup sugar |
| ½ tsp. vanilla |
| Pinch of salt |
| 3 eggs |
| 3 tbs. milk |
| 3¾ cups plus 1 tbs. flour |
| 1 tbs. baking powder |
| For frying: |
| 2 lbs. (6⅔ cups) oil |
| For coating: |
| 2 tbs. sugar |

In a mixing bowl use an electric mixer to beat the butter with the sugar, vanilla, salt, eggs, milk, 3 tablespoons of water, half the flour and the baking powder. Beat 2 minutes at the highest speed. • Add the remaining flour and quickly knead by hand. • Heat the oil to 350°. (The correct temperature has been reached when bubbles form quickly on a wooden spoon handle immersed in the oil.) On a floured surface roll out the dough ¼ inch thick and cut out 2 x 4-inch strips with a pastry cutter. Roll the pastry cutter down the strips to slit a hole in the center. Pull one end of the dough through the hole. • Drop 4 doughnuts at a time in the hot oil and fry on both sides until golden brown for about 3 to 4 minutes. • Lift the doughnuts out of the oil with a slotted spoon and drain on absorbent paper. Roll in the sugar while still warm.

# Dutch Raisin Doughnuts

### A regional specialty, easy to make

Preparation time: 40 minutes
Rising time: about 1¼ hours
Frying time: about 1 hour

| Makes 26 doughnuts |
| --- |
| 3¾ cups plus 1 tbs. flour |
| 1 packet dry yeast |
| ⅓ cup plus 2 tbs. sugar |
| 1 cup lukewarm milk |
| ¼ cup diced candied orange rind |
| ¾ cup raisins |
| ¾ cup currants |
| 1 tsp. vanilla |
| Pinch of salt |
| ⅓ cup softened butter |
| Grated rind of 1 orange |
| For frying: |
| 2 lbs. (6⅔ cups) oil |

| For the glaze: |
| --- |
| 2 cups powdered sugar |
| 2 tbs. rum or orange brandy |

Pour the flour into a bowl and make a well in the middle. Add the yeast into the well and mix with a little of the sugar, milk and flour. Cover and set aside 15 minutes to form the sponge. • Finely dice the candied orange rind. Wash the raisins and currants in hot water and drain on a kitchen towel. Mix the remaining sugar and milk with the vanilla, salt, butter and orange rind. Add to the yeast sponge and knead together with the flour. Knead in the candied and dried fruit. Let rise 30 minutes or until the dough has become substantially larger. • Cut 26 doughnuts from the dough with a large spoon and let these rise on a kitchen towel 30 minutes longer. • Heat the oil to

350°. • Fry the doughnuts on all sides to a golden brown for about 5 minutes. • For the glaze mix the powdered sugar with the rum or orange brandy and brush onto the doughnuts. Dry on a cake rack and enjoy them while fresh.

# Cinnamon Doughnuts

### Easy to make

Preparation time: 30 minutes
Baking time: 1½ hours

| Makes 40 doughnuts |
| --- |
| 7 tbs. butter |
| ⅔ cup sugar |
| 1 tsp. vanilla |
| ½ package powdered vanilla pudding mix |
| 2 eggs |
| 4 tbs. sour cream |

| 3½ cups flour |
| --- |
| 1½ tsp. baking powder |
| For frying: |
| 2 lbs. (6⅔ cups) oil |
| For coating: |
| 5 tbs. sugar |
| ½ tsp. cinnamon |

Cream the butter with the sugar, vanilla, and vanilla pudding mix. Add the eggs and sour cream. Mix the flour with the baking powder and stir into the first mixture a little at a time. Knead well. • On a floured surface roll the dough out ½-inch thick and cut out rings. Heat the oil to 350°. Fry the rings on both sides until golden brown, about 3 to 4 minutes. Drain on absorbent paper. • Mix the sugar with the cinnamon in a shallow bowl and roll the doughnuts in the mixture.

# Festive Cakes, Tortes and Tarts

## Lemon Tart

### Easy to make

Preparation time: 1 hour
Chilling time: 30 minutes
Baking time: 30 minutes

Ingredients for a 9-inch tart or springform pan

For the dough:

2⅓ cups flour

1 tbs. sugar

Pinch of salt

⅔ cup  chilled butter

1 egg

For the custard:

1 egg

⅓ cup plus 2 tbs. sugar

¾ cup plus 1 tbs. ground almonds

Juice of 1½ lemons

For the topping:

3 lemons

1 vanilla bean

1½ cups sugar

Cut the butter into flakes and quickly knead with the flour, sugar, salt and egg. Chill 30 minutes. • Preheat the oven to 400°. Line the pan with the rolled out dough, shaping a 1-inch rim. Bake the cake 15 minutes on the lower rack of the oven. • Beat the egg with the sugar. Add the almonds and enough lemon juice to make a thick paste. Spread the filling in the crust and bake 15 minutes on the middle rack of the oven. • Wash the lemons in hot water and cut into thin slices. Slit the vanilla bean lengthwise and scrape out the marrow. Bring this to a boil with the sugar in 1½ cups of water. Simmer the lemon slices in the sugar water for 10 to 15 minutes. Drain and arrange on the cooled tart. Cook the juice down until it gels and pour over the lemons.

## Orange Tart

### Easy to make

Preparation time: 1 hour
Chilling time: 30 minutes
Baking time: 40-45 minutes

Ingredients for a 9-inch tart or springform pan

For the dough:

2 cups flour

1 cup powdered sugar

⅔ cup butter

Pinch of salt

Grated rind of 1 lemon

For the custard:

3½ tbs. softened butter

2 eggs

⅓ cup plus 2 tbs. sugar

1 orange

1 tbs. cornstarch

For the topping:

3-4 oranges

2 tbs. orange marmalade

1-2 tbs. orange brandy

Quickly knead together the ingredients for the tart pastry with 2 tablespoons of cold water. Cover and chill 2 hours. • Preheat the oven to 400°. • Line a lightly buttered pan with the rolled out dough and bake 15 minutes. • Cream the butter and add the eggs and sugar. Grate the orange rind and squeeze the juice. Add the rind and juice to the custard. Pour the custard into the crust and bake 15 minutes longer. • Peel the oranges, removing the rind and the white skin. Slice thinly and arrange on the thickened custard. Bake another 10 to 15 minutes. • Stir the marmalade with the brandy to a smooth consistency and pour over the hot fruit.

## St. Honoré Meringue Cake

**A famous recipe**

Preparation time: 20 minutes
Drying time: 5 hours
Time to put the cake together:
1½ hours

| Ingredients for a 10-inch springform pan |
| --- |
| For the meringue: |
| 4 egg whites |
| Pinch of salt |
| 1¼ cups plus 1 tbs. sugar |
| 1 tsp. vanilla |
| For the cream puff dough: |
| ½ cup water |
| 3½ tbs. butter |
| Pinch of salt |
| ½ cup plus 1 tbs. flour |
| 2 eggs |
| For the custard: |
| 2 tsp. gelatin |
| ⅓ cup plus 1 tbs. cornstarch |
| 4 egg yolks |
| 2 cups milk |
| ⅓ cup plus 2 tbs. sugar |
| 1 vanilla bean |
| ¾ cup whipping cream |
| 2 tbs. orange brandy |
| For the glazing sugar: |
| 4 cups water |
| 1¼ cups plus 1 tbs. sugar |

Preheat the oven to 200°. Line the pan with parchment or waxed paper. • Beat the egg whites with the salt, sugar and vanilla until very stiff. Place in a pastry bag and pipe into the pan in a spiral starting at the center. Dry the meringue in the oven 5 hours. • When this is done bring the water to a boil with the butter and salt. Stir in the flour and eggs to make a choux paste. • With a pastry bag pipe walnut-sized choux paste mounds on a greased baking sheet and bake 15 minutes at 400° to make cream puff rosettes. • Dissolve the gelatin in a little water. Whisk the egg yolks with the cornstarch and a little of the milk. Bring the remaining milk to a boil with the sugar, va-nilla bean and the marrow scraped from the inside of the bean. Stir in the egg yolk mixture and heat without boiling for a few more minutes, stirring constantly. Add the dissolved gelatin to the hot custard, then allow to cool. Whip the cream until stiff and fold into the cooled custard with the brandy. • Place the custard in a pastry bag. Fill the cream puff rosettes with the custard and use the rest to cover the meringue. • Boil the water and sugar 5 minutes in a small saucepan. • Dip the rosettes in the glaze and place on the cake.•

# Frankfurt Wreath

### A famous recipe

Preparation time: 1 hour
Baking time: 50 minutes

| Ingredients for 1 tube pan |
| --- |
| ⅔ cup bread crumbs |
| For the batter: |
| 1 cup plus 1 tbs. butter |
| 1 cup sugar |
| 5 eggs |
| 1 tbs. lemon juice |
| 2⅔ cups flour |
| 1¼ cups cornstarch |
| 1 tbs. baking powder |
| For the fillings: |
| 1 cup plus 1 tbs. butter |
| 2 cups plus 3 tbs. powdered sugar |
| 2 egg yolks |
| 1 tsp. vanilla |
| 7 oz. almond paste |
| 2 tbs. orange brandy |
| 1 cup orange marmalade |
| For the almond cracknel: |
| 2 tbs. butter |
| 1 cup chopped almonds |
| ⅓ cup sugar |
| 2 tangerines |

Preheat the oven to 350°. Butter the tube pan and sprinkle with the bread crumbs. • Cream the butter with the sugar. Add the eggs and lemon juice. Mix the flour with the cornstarch and baking powder and fold into the first mixture. Spread the batter in the pan and bake 50 minutes. • Turn off the heat and leave the cake in the oven 10 minutes longer, then remove and allow to cool. • To make the butter cream filling, cream the butter, then stir in the powdered sugar, egg yolks and vanilla. • Mix the almond paste with the brandy and add as much water as needed to make it spreadable. • To make the cracknel heat the butter, add the almonds and sugar and caramelize to a golden brown, stirring constantly. Allow to cool. • Cut the wreath into four layers. On the bottom layer spread one-third of the butter cream, on the second the orange

marmalade and on the third the almond paste mixture. Top with the fourth layer and frost the cake with the remaining butter cream. Sprinkle with the cracknel. • Garnish with small mounds of butter cream and sections of tangerine.

## Hazelnut Torte

### Somewhat difficult

Preparation time: 20 minutes
Baking time: 1½ hours
Time to put the cake together: 30 minutes

Ingredients for a 10-inch springform pan

1 cup (8-9) egg whites
2¼ cups sugar
2 tbs. lemon juice
1¾ cups ground hazelnuts
½ cup plus 1 tbs. cornstarch
15 oz. chocolate
½ tbs. gelatin

⅔ cup whipping cream
2 tbs. very finely ground sugar
1 tsp. vanilla

Preheat the oven to 350°. Line the pan with parchment or waxed paper. • Beat the egg whites until foamy, then drizzle in the sugar while whipping until very stiff. Fold in the lemon juice, nuts and cornstarch. • Spread one-fifth of the batter in the pan and bake 15 minutes on the lower rack of the oven. Remove the baked layer and repeat the process five times. • Cut the last layer into 12 pieces and thoroughly cool all the layers. • Melt the chocolate in a bowl set in hot water. Spread thinly on each layer and dip the pieces into the chocolate. While the chocolate is still liquid mark off 12 sections with radial lines on one of the layers. • Dissolve the gelatin in a little water. Whip the cream until stiff with the vanilla

and sugar. Warm the gelatin over low heat, then stir in 2 tablespoons of the cream. Return the mixture to the whipped cream and fold in. Spread two-thirds of the whipped cream on three of the layers and stack them. • Top with the marked layer and place a small mound of whipped cream on the wide end of each marked slice. Coat the outside of the cake with the remaining whipped cream. Place the torte pieces at an angle between and on the mounds of whipped cream.

## Almond-Mocha Torte

### Easy to make

Preparation time: 30 minutes
Baking time: 40 minutes
Time to put the cake together: 30 minutes

Ingredients for a 10-inch springform pan

⅔ cup softened butter
1 cup sugar
2 eggs
Pinch of salt
1¼ cups flour
¾ cup plus 1 tbs. cornstarch
2 tsp. baking powder
3 tbs. milk
1 cup sliced almonds
½ tbs. gelatin
2½ cups whipping cream
5 tsp. instant coffee
1 tsp. vanilla
4 tbs. superfine sugar
16 coffee beans

Cream the butter with the sugar. Separate 1 of the eggs and stir the egg yolk, the second egg, the salt, flour, cornstarch, baking powder and milk into the butter-sugar mixture. Whisk the egg white. • Preheat

the oven to 475°. • Spread one-fourth of the batter in the bottom of the pan. Cover with one-fourth of the egg white and almonds and bake 10 minutes on the lower rack of the oven to a golden brown. Remove the baked layer and repeat this process three times. • Cut 1 of the layers into sixteen pieces. • Dissolve the gelatin in 3 tablespoons of cold water. Whip the cream until stiff with the coffee, vanilla and sugar. Warm the gelatin over low heat and fold into the whipped cream. • Spread the torte layers with whipped cream and stack them. Coat the outside of the cake in cream and top with the torte pieces. Garnish with small mounds of whipped cream and the coffee beans.

## Butter Cream Cake

### Easy to make

Preparation time: 1¼ hours
Baking time: 40 minutes

| Ingredients for a 10-inch springform pan |
| --- |
| 5 eggs |
| Pinch of salt |
| 1½ cups sugar |
| 1 cup flour |
| 1 scant cup cornstarch |
| 1 tsp. baking powder |
| ⅔ cup blanched almonds |
| ¾ cup sugar |
| ½ cup water |
| 5 egg yolks |
| 1 cup plus 1 tbs. butter |
| 1⅓ cups strawberry jam |
| ½ cup toasted sliced almonds |
| 2 oz. bittersweet chocolate |

**S**eparate the eggs. Beat the egg whites until stiff with the salt and ⅓ cup of sugar. Beat the egg yolks with 5 tablespoons of warm water and the remaining sugar until lemon colored. Fold in the flour, cornstarch, baking powder and egg whites. • Preheat the oven to 300°. Bake the sponge cake 10 minutes, turn up the heat to 350° and bake 30 minutes longer. • Turn off the heat and leave the cake in the oven 15 minutes longer. Let the cake stand 1 day. • Finely grind the almonds. Boil the sugar in the water to make a syrup. • Beat the egg yolks until lemon colored. Stir in the syrup. Combine this with the butter and stir in the almonds. • Cut the sponge cake into 3 layers. Cover the 2 lower layers with the jam and spread with a thin layer of butter cream. • Top with the remaining cake layer and cover the entire cake with butter cream. Sprinkle the sides with the toasted almonds and the top with grated chocolate.

## Chocolate-Cream Cake

### Easy to make, inexpensive

Preparation time: 20 minutes
Baking time: 40 minutes
Standing time: 1 day
Time to put the cake together: 40 minutes

| Ingredients for a 9-inch springform pan |
| --- |
| 4 eggs |
| Pinch of salt |
| 1¼ cups plus 1 tbs. sugar |
| ¾ cup plus 1 tbs. flour |
| ¾ cup plus 1 tbs. cornstarch |
| 1 tsp. baking powder |
| 3 tsp. gelatin |
| ¾ cup whipping cream |
| 2 tbs. super fine sugar |
| 1⅓ cups peach jam |
| 2 tbs. powdered instant cocoa |
| 4 oz. chocolate sprinkles |

**P**repare a sponge cake as in the preceding recipe from the eggs, salt, sugar, flour, cornstarch and baking powder. Bake 10 minutes at 300° and 30 minutes at 350°. Allow the cake to stand 1 day, then cut into three layers. • Dissolve the gelatin in a little cold water. • Whip the cream and sugar until stiff. In a small saucepan warm the dissolved gelatin over low heat. Stir in 3 tablespoons of the cream and fold the mixture into the remaining whipped cream. Place a little of the whipped cream in a pastry bag. • Cover the two bottom layers of the cake with the jam and spread with half the whipped cream which is not in the pastry bag. Stack the layers. • Mix the cocoa with the remaining whipped cream and use it to cover the cake. Garnish the sides with chocolate sprinkles and the top with small mounds of whipped cream.

## Black Forest Cake

### A famous recipe

Preparation time: 20 minutes
Baking time: 45 minutes
Standing time: at least 3 hours
Time to put the cake together:
45 minutes

| Ingredients for a 9-inch springform pan |
| --- |
| 4 oz. bittersweet chocolate |
| ⅔ cup butter |
| 1 cup sugar |
| ½ tsp. vanilla |
| 4 eggs |
| ⅓ cup plus 1 tbs. ground almonds |
| ⅓ cup plus 1 tbs. flour |
| ⅓ cup plus 1 tbs. cornstarch |
| ½ cup bread crumbs |
| 1 tbs. baking powder |
| For the filling: |
| 4 tbs. cherry liqueur |
| 2½ tsp. gelatin |
| 1 lb. sour cherries |
| 2 tbs. lemon juice |
| 2½ cups whipping cream |
| 2 tbs. super fine sugar |

**S**have 2 tablespoons of chocolate and melt the rest. • Cream the butter with the sugar and vanilla. • Separate the eggs. Mix the almonds with the flour, cornstarch, bread crumbs and baking powder. • Stir the egg yolks and the cooled melted chocolate into the butter-sugar mixture. Beat the egg whites until stiff and fold in with the dry ingredients. • Preheat the oven

to 350°. Bake the cake 45 minutes on the lower rack of the oven. Allow to stand at least 3 hours, then cut into three layers and sprinkle with the cherry liqueur. • Dissolve the gelatin in a little cold water. Wash and pit the cherries, then simmer 7 minutes in ½ cup of water and the lemon juice, remove and drain. • Whip the cream and sugar until stiff.

Warm the gelatin over low heat, then stir in a few tablespoons of the whipped cream. Return the mixture to the whipped cream and fold together. • Cover the first and second cake layers with the cooled cherries and whipped cream, set the third layer on top and cover the cake with the remaining whipped cream. Sprinkle with the chocolate shavings.

## Sachertorte

### A famous recipe

Preparation time: 20 minutes
Baking time: 45 minutes
Time to put the cake together:
20 minutes

Ingredients for a 9-inch
springform pan

5½ oz. bittersweet chocolate

½ cup plus 1 tbs. butter

5 eggs

¾ cup sugar

Pinch of salt

⅓ cup plus 1 tbs. flour

⅓ cup plus 1 tbs. cornstarch

1 tsp. baking powder

⅓ cup plus 1 tbs. ground
almonds

½ vanilla bean

⅔ cup cake or bread crumbs

⅔ cup apricot jam

8 oz. bittersweet chocolate

Melt the chocolate and butter in a bowl set in hot water. Separate the eggs. • Beat the egg yolks with the sugar until lemon colored. Beat the egg whites and salt until stiff. • Combine the flour, cornstarch, baking powder, ground almonds and the marrow scraped from the vanilla bean. Fold into the egg yolk-sugar mixture with the egg whites and the cooled melted chocolate. • Preheat the oven to 350°. Butter the pan and sprinkle with the crumbs. • Spread the batter in the pan and bake 45 minutes on the lower rack of the oven. • Turn off the heat and leave the cake in the oven 15 minutes longer. Heat the jam, stirring constantly, rub through a sieve and spread on the torte. Cover the cake with the melted chocolate and mark 12 slices in the glaze before it hardens.

## Linzer Torte

### Requires some time

Preparation time: 40 minutes
Chilling time: 30 minutes
Baking time: 45 minutes

Ingredients for a 9-inch
springform pan

1½ cups plus 1 tbs. flour

⅓ cup plus 1 tbs. cornstarch

½ cup plus 1 tbs. butter

¾ cup sugar

1 tsp. vanilla

1 egg

3 egg yolks

1 tsp. cinnamon

Generous pinch ground cloves

Generous pinch ground
cardamom

1 cup plus 2 tbs. ground
almonds

½ lemon

⅔ cup plus 3 tbs. apricot or
raspberry jam

1 tbs. apricot brandy or
raspberry liqueur

Cut the butter into small pieces and place in a bowl with the flour, cornstarch, sugar, vanilla, spices, almonds, egg and 2 of the egg yolks. Grate the lemon rind and mix with the squeezed juice. Quickly mix with the ingredients in the bowl to make a smooth pastry dough. • Cover and chill 30 minutes. • Stir the jam with the brandy or liqueur. • Preheat the oven to 350°. • Roll out two-thirds of the dough. Use it to line a pan, spreading the dough up the sides about 1-inch high. Spread with the jam. Roll out the remaining dough. Cut long strips with a pastry cutter and lay these in a lattice design over the jam. Brush with the remaining egg yolk. • Bake 45 minutes or until golden brown.

# Marzipan Torte

**Somewhat expensive, somewhat difficult**

Preparation time: 1 hour
Baking time: 1 hour
Time to put the cake together: 1 hour
Chilling time: 7 days

| Ingredients for an 11-inch springform pan |
| --- |
| ⅔ cup pistachios |
| 2 cups almonds |
| 10½ oz. almond paste |
| 8 cups powdered sugar |
| 10 eggs |
| 2 cups butter |
| Grated rind of 1 lemon |
| ⅔ cup lemon jam |
| 1 cup flour |
| 1 cup cornstarch |
| 4 oz. bittersweet chocolate |

Grind two-thirds of the pistachios. Pour boiling water over the almonds. Cool somewhat and remove the skins. Rub dry and grind. • Cut 7 oz. of the almond paste into small pieces and knead with 1 cup of the powdered sugar and the ground pistachios. Divide into 4 parts and set aside. • Preheat the oven to 475°. Butter the pan. • Separate the eggs. Sift 6¼ cups of powdered sugar over the butter and beat thoroughly. Add the egg yolks one at a time and add the lemon rind. Mix the flour with cornstarch and ground almonds. Beat the egg whites until stiff and fold into the butter mixture with the almond-flour mixture. • Place 2 tablespoons of the batter in the pan and spread evenly with a pastry brush. Bake to a golden brown in 5 minutes. • Add two more tablespoons of batter and bake as before. Re-

peat the process one more time, then spread the cake with 1 tablespoon lemon jam. Roll out 1 part of the pistachio marzipan between sheets of waxed paper to the size of the pan and lay this on the lemon jam. Spread two more tablespoons of batter in the pan and bake 5 more minutes. • Bake 3 more layers of cake, then a layer of jam and a layer of marzipan. Repeat these procedures until all the batter and marzipan have been used. After adding the second layer of marzipan begin baking the cake on the middle rack of the oven. • Allow the torte to cool somewhat, then remove from the pan and cool on a cake rack. • Cover the entire torte with the remaining lemon jam. • Knead the remaining marzipan with the remaining powdered sugar. Roll out a thin circle the size of the

top of the cake and a strip the width of the sides. With the help of waxed paper apply these to the cake. • Melt the chocolate and pour over the cake beginning at the center and working outward toward the edges. • Chop the remaining pistachios and sprinkle on the cake. Mark slices with radial lines while the chocolate is still soft. • Wrap loosely in waxed paper and aluminum foil and chill at least 7 days before cutting.

Tip: This torte stays fresh even after it has been cut if it is kept wrapped and chilled. The flavor grows stronger with time.

## Dutch Cherry Cake

### A famous recipe

Preparation time: 1¾ hours
Baking time: 30 minutes

| | |
|---|---|
| ⅔ lb. frozen puff pastry | |
| ½ cup sliced almonds | |
| 1 lb. dark cherries | |
| 4 tbs. sugar | |
| ½ tsp. cinnamon | |
| 1 tbs. cornstarch | |
| 2 tbs. currant jelly | |
| 1 cup plus 2 tbs. powdered sugar | |
| 1-2 tbs. cherry liqueur | |
| 1 tbs. plus ½ tsp. gelatin | |
| 3 cups whipping cream | |
| ½ tsp. vanilla | |

Thaw the puff pastry. • Toast the sliced almonds. Wash, dry and pit the cherries and simmer 7 minutes with ½ cup water, 2 tbs. sugar and the cinnamon. Stir a little water into the cornstarch, then add to the cherries. Bring to a boil and cool. • Preheat the oven to 400°. • Roll out the puff pastry and cut out three 10-inch circles. Lay on a baking sheet rinsed with cold water and bake 10 minutes to a pale gold color. • Spread one of the cooled layers with the jelly. Stir the powdered sugar with the cherry liqueur and pour over the jelly. Allow to dry. • Dissolve the gelatin in a little cold water. Whip the cream with the remaining sugar and vanilla. • Warm the gelatin over low heat, then stir 3 tablespoons of the whipped cream into the gelatin. Return the mixture to the whipped cream and fold together. • Spread the cherries on one of the plain pastry layers and cover with whipped cream. Cover with the second pastry layer and then a thick layer of whipped cream. Cut the glazed pastry layer into 12 pieces and arrange on the whipped cream. • Spread the sides with whipped cream and sprinkle with the toasted almonds.

## Carrot Torte

**A Swiss specialty**

Preparation time: 30 minutes
Baking time: 50 minutes
Standing time: 1 day
Time to put the cake together:
30 minutes

Ingredients for a 10-inch
springform pan

⅔ lb. carrots

5 eggs

1¼ cups plus 1 tbs. sugar

1 tsp. vanilla

2⅓ cups ground almonds

1 tsp. cinnamon

Generous pinch of cloves

Generous pinch of freshly grated
nutmeg

2 tbs. rum

⅔ cup bread crumbs

4 oz. almond paste

2½ cups powdered sugar

12 pistachios

Several drops red food coloring

About 2 tbs. lemon juice

**P**eel, wash and grate the carrots. • Separate the eggs. Beat the egg yolks with the sugar and vanilla until lemon colored. Beat the egg whites until stiff. Mix the carrots, almonds, spices and rum with the egg yolks. Fold in the egg whites. • Preheat the oven to 400°. Butter the pan well and sprinkle with the bread crumbs. • Spread the batter in the pan and bake the torte 50 minutes. Allow to stand 1 day. • Knead the almond paste with ½ cup of the powdered sugar and mix in the coloring a drop at a time. Shape 12 little carrots and insert split pistachios in the ends. • Make a glaze with the remaining powdered sugar and lemon juice and pour over the cake.

## Wachau Chocolate Torte

**An Austrian specialty**

Preparation time: 30 minutes
Baking time: 45 minutes
Standing time: 1 day
Time to put the cake together:
30 minutes

Ingredients for a 10-inch
springform pan

¾ heaping cup almonds

10 oz. bittersweet chocolate

7 eggs

¾ cup sugar

2 tbs. rum

2 tsp. gelatin

2 cups whipping cream

½ tsp. vanilla

1 tbs. superfine sugar

12 chocolate leaves

**G**rind the almonds and grate the chocolate. • Preheat the oven to 350°. Line the bottom and sides of the pan with parchment or waxed paper. • Separate 3 of the eggs. Beat the 4 whole eggs with the 3 egg yolks until lemon colored adding the sugar a little at a time. Beat the egg whites until stiff. • Add the egg whites, almonds and 6 oz. chocolate to the egg-sugar mixture and gently fold in with a whisk. Bake 45 minutes on the lower rack of the oven. • Cool the torte on a cake rack, and cut into 3 layers and allow to stand 1 day. • Melt the remaining chocolate in a bowl set in hot water. Pour over the top layer and mark 12 slices in the chocolate. Sprinkle the other two layers with the rum. Dissolve the gelatin in a little cold water. Whip the cream with the vanilla and sugar. Warm the gelatin over low heat and stir in a couple of tablespoons of

whipped cream. Return the mixture to the whipped cream and fold together. • Spread the whipped cream mixture over the 2 layers and then stack these layers with the chocolate covered layer on top. Garnish with the chocolate leaves.

## Banana Torte

### Nutritious whole-wheat recipe

Preparation time: 15 minutes
Baking time: 25 minutes
Time to put the cake together: 1½ hours

| Ingredients for a 10-inch springform pan |
| --- |
| 4 eggs |
| 1 cup unrefined cane sugar |
| ¾ cup plus 1 tbs. cup whole-wheat flour |
| ⅓ cup cocoa |
| 1 tsp. baking powder |
| 1 tsp. cinnamon |
| 1 lb. bananas |
| 3½ tbs. butter |
| ⅓ cup honey |
| ¾ cup plus 1 tbs. rice flour |
| ½ tsp. cinnamon |
| 2 tbs. rum |
| ¾ cup whipping cream |
| ½ tsp. vanilla |
| ¼ cup dried bananas |
| 6 maraschino cherries |
| 2 oz. bittersweet chocolate |

**P**reheat the oven to 400°. • Separate the eggs and beat the egg yolks well with ⅔ cup of the sugar and 2 tablespoons of warm water. Mix the whole-wheat flour with the cocoa, baking powder and cinnamon and fold into the egg-sugar mixture. Beat the egg whites until stiff and fold in. • Bake the cake 25 minutes, cool and cut into two layers. • Slice the peeled bananas. Bring 1 cup of water to a boil with the butter and honey. Add the rice flour and bananas and cook 5 minutes, stirring constantly. Remove from the heat and add the cinnamon and rum. Spread on the bottom layer of cake and cool. • Whip the cream until stiff with the remaining sugar and vanilla and spread about ⅓ on the filling. Top with the second layer and cover the cake with the remaining whipped cream. Decorate the torte with the dried banana pieces, cherries and shaved chocolate.

## Old Vienna Punch Torte

### An Austrian specialty

Preparation time: 20 minutes
Baking time: 45 minutes
Standing time: 2 days
Time to put the cake together: 1 hour

| Ingredients for a 9-inch springform pan |
| --- |
| 6 eggs |
| ¾ cup sugar |
| 1¼ cups flour |
| ½ cup plus 1 tbs. cornstarch |
| 2 tsp. baking powder |
| 6 tbs. rum |
| 1 cup apricot jam |
| Juice of 2 oranges |
| Juice of 1 lemon |
| 2 cups powdered sugar |
| ½ tsp. cocoa |

**P**reheat the oven to 350°. • Separate the eggs. Beat the egg whites until stiff and cream the yolks with ⅔ cup of the sugar. Fold in the egg whites, flour, cornstarch and baking powder. • Bake the sponge cake 45 minutes. Allow to stand 1 day, then cut into three layers. Cut the middle layer into 1-inch cubes and sprinkle the other layers with 1 tablespoon of rum and spread with ⅔ cup of the jam. • Place the bottom layer in the springform pan again. Bring to a boil 1 tablespoon of the rum with the juices, 3 tablespoons of jam and the remaining sugar. Stir in the sponge cake cubes and spread the mixture on the bottom layer. Cover with the top layer and press down gently. • Set a flat circular board on the cake, weigh it down and allow to stand 1 hour. Warm the remaining jam and pour over the cake. • Mix the powdered sugar with the remaining rum and mix 2 tablespoons of the icing with the cocoa and place in a pastry bag. • Frost the cake with the plain icing, then pipe the cocoa icing onto the cake in a spiral and draw radial lines from the center through the spiral with a knife.

## Walnut Torte

**Nutritious whole-wheat recipe**

Preparation time: 30 minutes
Baking time: 35 minutes
Time to put the cake together: 1½ hours

| Ingredients for an 11-inch springform pan |
| For the batter: |
| ¾ cup whole toasted walnuts |
| 2 cups whole-wheat flour |
| ½ cup cocoa |
| 2 tsp. baking powder |
| ¾ cup softened butter |
| ¾ cup honey |
| 4 eggs |
| 2 tbs. rum |
| For the filling and topping: |
| 2 cups whole walnuts |
| ¾ cup plus 1 tbs. whole-wheat flour |
| ½ tsp. cinnamon |
| ½ tsp. vanilla |
| ⅓ cup plus 1 tbs. honey |
| 7 tbs. butter |
| 1 cup milk |
| 4 tbs. walnut brandy |
| 1½ cups whipping cream |

| 2 tbs. unrefined granulated cane sugar |
| ½ tsp. vanilla |
| 16 walnut halves |

Grate the nuts and mix with the flour, cocoa and baking powder. • Cream the butter with the honey and stir in the flour mixture alternately with the eggs and rum. • Preheat the oven to 350°. Grease the pan. • Bake the torte 35 minutes. • For the filling, chop half the nuts and toast with the flour. Add the spices, honey, butter and milk, and cook until thickened. • Cut the torte into 2 layers and sprinkle with 2 tablespoons of brandy. • Mix the remaining brandy with the filling and spread on the bottom layer. Set the second layer on top and press down gently. • Cool the torte. • Grind the remaining nuts. Whip the cream with the sugar and vanilla until stiff and add the ground nuts. Spread over the top and sides of the torte and top with the walnut halves.

## Persimmon Tart

### Somewhat expensive

Preparation time: 20 minutes
Chilling time: 30 minutes
Baking time: 20 minutes
Time to put the cake together:
30 minutes

| Ingredients for a 10-inch springform pan |
| --- |
| 1⅓ cups flour |
| ⅓ cup plus 1 tbs. ground almonds |
| ¾ cup plus 1 tsp. powdered sugar |
| 7 tsp. chilled butter |
| For the filling: |
| 7 tsp. softened butter |
| 2 tbs. egg wash |
| 3 tsp. powdered sugar |
| 1 tsp. vanilla extract |
| 4-5 persimmons |
| ¼ cup apricot jam |
| 1 tbs. Cointreau |
| ¾ cup whipping cream |
| 1 tbs. sugar |
| 1 tbs. chopped pistachios |

**M**ix the flour with the almonds and powdered sugar. Cut the butter into pieces over the flour and quickly knead into a smooth pastry dough. Chill 30 minutes. • On a floured surface roll out the dough. Lightly butter the bottom of the springform pan and line with the pastry, spreading the dough up the sides about 1-inch high. • Bake 20 minutes on the middle rack of a 400° oven. • Cool in the pan. • Beat the butter with the egg wash, the powdered sugar and vanilla. Spread the butter cream in the pie crust. Peel the persimmons, slice thinly and arrange on the custard. Stir the jam with the Cointreau, warm briefly, allow to cool somewhat and pour over the persimmons. • Whip the cream and sugar until stiff and use it to decorate the tart. Sprinkle with the chopped pistachios.

## Raspberry Ice-Cream Cake

### Requires some time

Preparation time: 40 minutes
Standing time: 1 day
Baking time: 35 minutes
Chilling time: 6 hours

Ingredients for a 9-inch springform pan

4 eggs

Pinch of salt

1¾ cups plus 1 tbs. sugar

¾ cup plus 1 tbs. flour

¾ cup plus 1 tbs. cornstarch

1 tsp. baking powder

½ lb. raspberries

2 tsp. raspberry liqueur

1½ cups whipping cream

1 tbs. powdered sugar

Separate the eggs and beat the egg whites until stiff with the salt and ⅓ cup of the sugar.

Beat the egg yolks with 4 tablespoons of warm water, drizzling in 1 cup of the sugar. Fold in the egg whites, flour, cornstarch and baking powder. • Preheat the oven to 350°. • Bake the sponge cake 35 minutes, then allow to stand 24 hours. • Pour the raspberry liqueur over the raspberries. • Cut the cake into 2 layers and return the bottom layer to the pan. • Whip the cream until stiff, drizzling in the remaining sugar. Place 4 tablespoons of the whipped cream in a pastry bag with a flower tip. • Drain the raspberries and set aside 12 berries for decoration. Mix the remaining berries with the whipped cream. Spread the whipped cream on the bottom layer. • Top with the second layer and press down gently. Sift powdered sugar over the cake and decorate with small mounds of whipped cream with a raspberry in the center of each. • Chill 6 hours.

## Chilled Yogurt Tart

### Requires some time

Preparation time: 2 hours
Chilling time: about 6 hours

Ingredients for an 11-inch springform pan

1¾ cups flour

7 tbs. butter

1 egg yolk

Pinch of salt

⅓ cup sugar

½ tsp. vanilla

2 packages unflavored gelatin

2 cups whole milk yogurt

⅔ cup sugar

Grated rind of ½ lemon

2 tsp. lemon juice

1½ cups whipping cream

2 tbs. pineapple juice

½ pineapple

5½ oz. frozen raspberries

Knead the butter with the egg yolk, flour, salt, sugar and vanilla. Chill the pastry dough 1 hour, then roll out. Line the pan with the pastry, prick well with a fork and bake 20 minutes. • Dissolve 1 package gelatin in a little water. • Mix the yogurt with the sugar, lemon rind and lemon juice. Whip the cream until stiff. • Heat the pineapple juice. Add the dissolved gelatin and gradually stir in the yogurt. Chill briefly to thicken and fold in the whipped cream. • Spread the filling in the cooled pie crust and chill until the surface has stiffened. • Peel the pineapple and cut into thin slices. • Prepare the second package gelatin following package directions. • Arrange the fruit on the tart and pour on the glaze. • Chill the yogurt tart 5 hours to stiffen.

## Cornflake Cake

### Somewhat difficult

Preparation time: 1½ hours
Chilling time: 1 hour

| Ingredients for a 9-inch springform pan |
| --- |
| 7 tbs. butter |
| 5½ oz. bittersweet chocolate |
| ⅔ cup cornflakes |
| 1 tsp. gelatin |
| ⅔ cup sugar |
| 2 egg yolks |
| Juice of 1 lemon |
| 1 cup ricotta or cottage cheese |
| 1½ cups whipping cream |
| 1½ cups pitted sweet cherries |
| 2 tbs. shaved chocolate |

**M**elt the butter with the chocolate and stir in the cornflakes. • Spread a sheet of parchment or waxed paper with butter. Set 12 mounds of corn-flake mixture on the paper. • Line the bottom and sides of the pan with parchment or waxed paper. Spread the remaining cornflake mixture in the pan and press down firmly. Chill the corn-flake-mounds and the pan. • Dissolve the gelatin in a little cold water. • Beat the sugar with the egg yolks until lemon colored, then add the lemon juice and cheese. • Whip the cream until stiff. • Warm the gelatin in a small saucepan over low heat. Stir a few tablespoons of the cheese into the gelatin and re-turn this mixture to the cheese, then fold into the whipped cream. • Spread one-third of the cheese-cream mixture on the cornflake crust. Spread the cher-ries on the cheese cream and top with the remaining cheese cream. Chill at least 1 hour. • Decorate with the cornflake mounds and the shaved choco-late.

## Potato Cake

### A specialty, easy to make

Preparation time: 1 hour
Baking time: 50 minutes
Time to put the cake together: 10 minutes

| Ingredients for a 10-inch springform pan |
| --- |
| ⅔ lb. potatoes cooked the day before |
| 1¼ cups whole hazelnuts |
| ⅓ cup raisins |
| 2 tbs. rum |
| 4 eggs |
| 1¼ cups plus 1 tbs. sugar |
| ¾ cup plus 1 tbs. flour |
| ⅓ cup plus 1 tbs. cornstarch |
| 2 tsp. baking powder |
| Grated rind of 1 lemon |
| ½ tsp. cinnamon |
| ⅔ cup  bread crumbs |
| 2 cups powdered sugar |
| 2 tbs. rum |
| 3 tbs. currant jelly |
| 8 marzipan potatoes |

**P**eel the potatoes and press through a potato ricer or grate. Grind the nuts. Wash the raisins in hot water, drain and sprinkle with the rum. • Separate the eggs and beat the yolks with the sugar until lemon colored. Mix the flour with the cornstarch and baking powder. Stir into the egg-sugar mixture with the lemon rind, cinnamon, potatoes, nuts and raisins. Beat the egg whites until stiff and fold in. • Preheat the oven to 400°. Butter the pan and sprinkle with the bread crumbs. • Spread the bat-ter evenly in the pan. Bake 50 minutes, then turn down the heat and leave the torte in the oven 10 minutes longer. • Stir the powdered sugar with the rum, currant jelly and 1 table-

spoon water to a smooth consistency, then pour over the torte to glaze. • Garnish the torte with the marzipan potatoes.

## Raspberry-Cream Cake

### Requires some time

Preparation time: 30 minutes
Baking time: 30 minutes
Standing time: at least 6 hours
Time to put the cake together: 45 minutes

| Ingredients for a 10-inch springform pan |
| --- |
| ⅔ cup bread crumbs |
| For the sponge cake: |
| 6 eggs |
| Pinch of salt |
| 1 cup sugar |
| 1⅓ cups flour |
| ½ cup plus 1 tsp. cornstarch |
| 2 tsp. baking powder |
| For the filling and garnish: |
| ½ cup sliced almonds |
| 1 tbs. gelatin |
| 1 cup low-fat yogurt |
| Grated rind of ½ lemon |
| 3 tbs. maple syrup |
| 2 tbs. sugar |
| 1 tsp. vanilla |
| 2 cups whipping cream |
| 1 tsp. lemon juice |
| 1⅓ lbs. raspberries |
| 2 tbs. powdered sugar |
| ½ cup raspberry jam |
| 2 tbs. raspberry liqueur |
| 2 tbs. chopped pistachios |

**P**reheat the oven to 350°. Butter the bottom of the pan and sprinkle with the bread crumbs. • Separate the eggs. Beat the egg whites with the salt until stiff. Beat the egg yolks with the sugar until the sugar is completely dissolved. Add the egg whites to the yolk-sugar mixture. Sift the flour with the cornstarch and baking powder and fold the flour mixture into the yolk-sugar mixture. • Spread the batter evenly in the pan and bake 30 minutes on the middle rack of the oven to a golden brown. Turn out onto a cake rack and allow to rest. • Toast the almonds in a dry pan stirring constantly and allow to cool. • Dissolve the gelatin in a little water. Stir the yogurt with the lemon rind, maple syrup, sugar and vanilla. Whip the cream until stiff and fold half the whipped cream into the yogurt. • Heat the lemon juice with 2 tablespoons of water and add the dissolved gelatin. Stir the yogurt into half the gelatin a little at a time. Stir the remaining gelatin into the whipped cream. • Wash and pat the raspberries dry, reserving some for decoration. Puree the raspberries with the powdered sugar. • Place one-third of the whipped cream in a pastry bag with a flower tip. Mix the rest with the raspberry puree. • Cut the sponge cake into two layers. Stir the jam with the raspberry liqueur and spread on the bottom layer. Spread with the yogurt, top with the second layer and press down gently. • Spread the top and sides of the cake with raspberry cream and sprinkle with sliced almonds. • Arrange the reserved raspberries on the cake, place mounds of whipped cream around the edge and sprinkle with chopped pistachios. • Chill the cake.

## American Cake

**Requires some time, a regional specialty**

Preparation time: 40 minutes
Baking time: 50 minutes

Ingredients for a 10-inch springform pan

For the batter:

| ½ cup plus 1 tbs. butter |
| 2 cups plus 1 tbs. sugar |
| 4 eggs |
| 2 cups plus 1 tbs. flour |
| 2 tsp. baking powder |
| 2 tbs. milk |

For the filling:

| 3 lemons |
| ⅔ cup sugar |
| 3 tsp. cornstarch |
| 2 cups whipping cream |

Cream the butter with ¾ cup of the sugar. Separate the eggs and fold the egg yolks into the butter-sugar mixture with the flour, baking powder and milk. • Preheat the oven to 400°. • Bake half the batter 15 minutes. • Beat the egg whites with the remaining sugar until very stiff. Spread half the egg-sugar mixture on the baked cake layer. Bake 10 minutes longer. Bake the remaining batter and egg-sugar mixture in the same way. • Allow the cake layers to cool. • Squeeze the lemons. Stir the juice with ½ cup water and the sugar and allow to boil. Stir in the cornstarch mixed with a little cold water. Bring to a boil and then cool. • Whip the cream until very stiff and stir in the cold lemon pudding 1 tablespoon at a time. Spread half the lemon cream on one of the cake layers and cover with the second layer and the remaining cream. • Serve the cake immediately.

## Wedding Torte

**A festive specialty**

Preparation time: 1½ hours
Baking time: 45 minutes

Ingredients for a 10-inch springform pan

For the batter:

| 1 cup plus 2 tbs. softened butter |
| ¾ cup sugar |
| ½ tsp. vanilla |
| 4 eggs |
| 1¼ cups flour |
| 1¼ cups cornstarch |
| ¾ cup plus 1 tsp. ground blanched almonds |
| 2 tsp. baking powder |

For the custard:

| ½ cup butter |
| ¾ cup sugar |
| 4 egg yolks |
| 2 tbs. lemons |

For the glaze and garnish:

| 1 egg white |
| 2½ cups powdered sugar |
| 1 tbs. lemon juice |
| 2 tbs. chopped pistachios |
| 16 candied violets |

Cream the butter with the sugar and vanilla. Beat in the eggs and 4 tablespoons water. • Stir in the flour, cornstarch, almonds and baking powder. • Preheat the oven to 350°. • Bake the torte 45 minutes. • Melt the butter. Add the sugar and the egg yolks. Grate the rind of 1 of the lemons and squeeze the juice of both lemons. Stir the rind and juice into the custard. Beat in a bowl set in hot water and allow to cool. • Cut the torte into three layers. Spread 2 of the layers with the lemon custard and stack the layers. • Beat the egg white with the powdered sugar and lemon juice. Pour over the cake. Garnish with pistachios and candied violets.

## Cheese Cake with Mango

**Somewhat expensive**

Preparation time: 2¼ hours
Baking time: 20 minutes

| |
|---|
| Ingredients for an 11-inch springform pan |
| 3 eggs |
| ⅓ cup sugar |
| ½ tsp. vanilla |
| ⅓ cup plus 1 tbs. flour |
| 3 tbs. cornstarch |
| 3½ tsp. ground hazelnuts |
| 2 tsp. gelatin |
| 2 cups ricotta or cottage cheese |
| 2 cups cream cheese |
| ⅔ cup sugar |
| ⅔ cup yogurt |
| 4 tbs. egg wash |
| 1 lemon |
| 2½ cups whipping cream |
| 1 tbs. amaretto |
| 1 large mango |
| 4 kiwis |

**P**reheat the oven to 350°. • Separate the eggs and beat the egg whites until stiff. Beat the egg yolks with the sugar and vanilla until lemon colored. Fold the flour, cornstarch, nuts and egg whites into the egg-sugar mixture. Bake the sponge cake 20 minutes. • Dissolve the gelatin in a little water. • Beat the drained cheese with the cream cheese, sugar, yogurt and egg wash. Grate the lemon rind into the cheese mixture. • Squeeze the lemon juice, heat with 2 tablespoons of water and add the dissolved gelatin. Gradually add the cheese mixture and chill until partially stiff. • Whip the cream until stiff and fold in. • Sprinkle the sponge cake with the amaretto and replace in the pan. Cover the sides with waxed paper. • Peel the mango and cut from the pit in thin slices. Peel the kiwis and cut in half. Arrange the fruit alternately on the cake layers. Spread the cheese mixture on the torte layers and chill 4 hours.

## Vanilla Cake

### Nutritious whole-wheat recipe

Preparation time: 20 minutes
Baking time: 35 minutes
Time to put the cake together:
1½ hours

| Ingredients for a 10-inch springform pan |
| --- |
| 5 eggs |
| ½ tsp. vanilla |
| 1 cup unrefined cane sugar |
| ¾ cup plus 1 tbs. whole-wheat flour |
| 3½ tsp. cornstarch |
| 1 tsp. baking powder |
| 4 oz. coarsely grated bittersweet chocolate |
| ⅓ cup melted butter |
| 1⅓ cups blanched almonds |
| ½ cup honey |
| 1 tbs. rose water |
| 3 cups milk |
| ⅓ cup plus 1 tsp. cornstarch |
| ½ tsp. vanilla |
| 1½ tsp. butter |
| 1 egg yolk |
| 12 currants |

To make the batter beat the egg yolks with the vanilla, sugar and 2 tablespoons of water. Mix the flour with the cornstarch, baking powder and chocolate. Beat the egg whites until stiff and fold in with the melted butter. • Preheat the oven to 350°. Bake for 35 minutes, then cool and cut into three layers. • Finely grind the almonds, and stir until smooth with ⅓ cup of the honey and the rose water in a bowl set in hot water. • Heat the remaining honey. • Combine the milk with the cornstarch and vanilla, stir into the honey and bring to a boil several times in succession. • Stir the butter and egg yolk into one-third of the pudding. Spread the remaining pudding while still warm on the 2 bottom layers of cake. Stack the layers. Spread the top layer with the butter-and-egg pudding mixture. • Shape

12 blossoms from half the marzipan and set on the cake. Set a currant in each blossom. Cover the sides with rolled out marzipan.

## Heaven Cake

### Requires some time

Preparation time: 40 minutes
Baking time: 1½ hours

Ingredients for a 10-inch springform pan

¾ cup softened butter

1¼ cups plus 2 tbs. sugar

3 eggs

2⅓ cups flour

2 tsp. baking powder

¾ cup plus 1 tsp. ground almonds

1½ tsp. vanilla

½ tsp. gelatin

3 cups whipping cream

**C**ream the butter with 1 cup of the sugar and the eggs. Stir in the flour and baking powder. • Preheat the oven to 350°. Butter the bottom of the pan. • Spread one-fourth of the batter in the pan and bake 10 minutes. • Mix the almonds with 2 tablespoons of the sugar and 1 teaspoon of the vanilla. Sprinkle on the baked cake layer and bake 15 minutes longer. • Repeat the process to make 3 more layers. • When it has baked 10 minutes cut the last layer into 12 slices return it to the oven and bake 5 minutes longer. • Dissolve the gelatin in 3 tablespoons of water. • Whip the cream until stiff with the remaining sugar and vanilla. Warm the gelatin over low heat and gradually combine with the whipped cream. Place one-third of the cream in a pastry bag. Spread the remaining cream on the 3 cake layers and stack the layers.

• Mark 12 slices with radial lines on the top layer and set small mounds of whipped cream between the marks. • Set the precut slices diagonally on and between the mounds of whipped cream.

## Black Bread Torte

### Easy to make and inexpensive

Preparation time: 40 minutes
Baking time: 40 minutes

Ingredients for a 10-inch springform pan

1½ cups seedless whole-rye bread

1 cup whole almonds

6 eggs

1⅓ cups sugar

1 tsp. baking powder

1 tbs. flour

2 tsp. rum or cherry liqueur

1½ cups whipping cream

1 lb. pitted sour cherries

**D**ice the bread and toast in a pan, turning constantly, but do not brown. Allow to cool. • Grind the almonds. Separate the eggs. Beat the egg yolks until lemon colored, drizzling in 1¼ cups plus 1 tbs. of the sugar. • Mix the baking powder with the flour and fold into the first mixture with the diced bread, ground almonds and rum or cherry liqueur. Beat the egg whites until stiff and fold into the batter. • Preheat the oven to 400°. Butter the pan well. • Spread the batter in the pan and bake 40 minutes. • Cool the cake. • Whip the cream with the remaining sugar until very stiff. Cut the torte into two layers. Spread 2 tablespoons of the whipped cream on the bottom layer and cover with the cherries,

reserving 12 cherries for garnish. Top with the second layer and frost the cake with ⅔ of the whipped cream. Using a pastry bag pipe small mounds of whipped cream around the top of the cake and garnish with cherries.

## Nut Torte with Lingonberry Cream

### Quick and easy to make

Preparation time: 25 minutes
Baking time: 40 minutes
Time to put the cake together: 40 minutes

Ingredients for a 10-inch springform pan

For the batter:

¾ cup softened butter

1 cup plus 1 tbs. sugar

½ tsp. vanilla

| 4 eggs |
| 2 cups ground hazelnuts |
| 2 tsp. baking powder |
| 4 oz. grated bittersweet chocolate |
| 2 tbs. cocoa |
| For the filling and garnish: |
| ½ tbs. gelatin |
| 1 lb. lingonberries |
| 1 cup whipping cream |

Cream the butter, sugar and vanilla, then add the eggs one at a time, the ground nuts, baking powder, 2½ ounces of the grated chocolate and the cocoa. • Preheat the oven to 350°. Butter the pan. • Bake the torte 40 minutes, then turn off the heat and leave the cake in the oven 10 minutes longer. • Cool the layers. • Dissolve the gelatin in a little cold water. Warm in a small saucepan over low heat and stir into the lingonberries. •

Whip the cream until stiff and combine half the whipped cream with the lingonberries. • Cut the torte into two layers and spread the bottom layer with the lingonberry cream. Set the second layer on top. • Spread the entire cake with whipped cream and sprinkle the sides with the remaining chocolate shavings. Decorate the top of the cake with mounds of whipped cream.

## Blueberry-Almond Tart

### Easy to make

Preparation time: 1 hour
Baking time: 40 minutes

Ingredients for a 10-inch springform pan

For the dough:

¾ cup plus 1 tsp. butter

| 1¼ cups plus 1 tbs. sugar |
| Pinch of salt |
| 2 eggs |
| Grated rind of 1 lemon |
| Generous pinch of ground cloves |
| Generous pinch of cinnamon |
| 1⅓ cups blanched almonds |
| 1½ cups plus 1 tbs. flour |
| For the filling: |
| 3½ tsp. softened butter |
| ⅓ cup plus 2 tbs. sugar |
| 2 tbs. raspberry liqueur |
| 1 tbs. lemon juice |
| 1¼ cups ground almonds |
| 1 egg white |
| ⅔ lb. blueberries |
| 1 egg yolk |
| 2 tbs. black currant jelly |

Cream the butter with the sugar and salt. Add the eggs one at a time, then gradually add the spices, almonds and

flour. • Line the bottom of the greased pan with half the dough and chill 30 minutes. • Knead the remaining dough with some flour. Roll half into a long strip and make 1-inch sides for the tart. • To make the filling, beat the butter with the sugar, raspberry liqueur, lemon juice and almonds. Beat the egg white until stiff and fold into the mixture. Spread the almond mixture on the crust and cover with the blueberries. Roll out the remaining dough, cut out ½-inch strips and lay these in radial lines from the center of the tart. Brush with the egg yolk. • Preheat the oven to 400°. • Bake the tart 40 minutes. • Stir the black currant jelly and spread on the hot berries.

## Malakow Torte

### A famous recipe, requires some time

Preparation time: 1½ hours
Baking time: 15 minutes
Chilling time: 2 hours

| Ingredients for a 9-inch springform pan |
| --- |
| For the batter: |
| 3 eggs |
| ⅓ cup sugar |
| Pinch of salt |
| ½ cup plus 1 tbs. flour |
| Generous pinch of baking powder |
| Grated rind of 1 lemon |
| For the filling and garnish: |
| ½ cup dry white wine |
| Juice of ½ orange |
| 3 tbs. sugar |
| 4 tsp. rum |
| 1½ cups sliced almonds |

| |
| --- |
| 1 cup plus 1 tsp. softened butter |
| 1¼ cups powdered sugar |
| 5 egg yolks |
| 4 oz. lady finger cookies |
| 1½ tsp. gelatin |
| 1½ cups whipping cream |

To make the sponge cake, separate the eggs and beat the egg yolks with 3 tablespoons of hot water. Gradually drizzle in the sugar and beat until the mixture is thick, white and creamy. • Whip the egg whites with the salt until stiff. Slide the egg whites into the egg yolk mixture, sift the flour and baking powder over both and fold in with the lemon rind. • Preheat the oven to 400°. Butter the bottom of the pan. • Spread the batter in the pan and bake 15 minutes on the middle rack of the oven to a golden brown. Cool on a cake rack. •

Meanwhile bring the white wine to a boil with the orange juice and 2 tablespoons of the sugar. Mix with the rum and allow to cool. • To make the butter cream toast the almonds in a dry pan until light brown, then place on a plate to cool. • Beat the butter, gradually adding the powdered sugar and egg yolks. Grind 1 cup of the almonds and blend with the butter cream. • Set the cake on a platter, place the springform rim around it, line the sides with a strip of parchment or waxed paper and spread the surface of the cake with 2 tablespoons of the butter cream. • Soak the lady fingers in the chilled wine-and-juice mixture and lay them on the cake facing in one direction. • Spread the cookies with butter cream; lay another layer of wine-soaked cookies in the other direction and cover with the rest of the

butter cream. Chill 2 hours. •
Carefully remove the springform
rim and parchment paper. •
Soak the gelatin in 2 tablespoons
of cold water, then warm over
low heat. Whip the cream with
the remaining sugar until stiff and
blend with the gelatin, 1 tablespoon at a time. Place one-third
of the whipped cream in a pastry
bag with a flower tip and cover
the cake with the remaining
whipped cream. Place small
mounds of whipped cream
around the top of the cake and
sprinkle with the remaining sliced
almonds.

Tip: From the remaining egg
whites make almond meringues
or macaroons.

## Lemon Cake

### Requires some time

Preparation time: 45 minutes
Chilling time: 12 hours
Baking time: 25 minutes
Time to put the cake together:
30 minutes
Chilling time: 2 hours

| Ingredients for a 9-inch springform pan |
| --- |
| For the cream: |
| Juice and grated rind of 1 lemon |
| ¾ cup sugar |
| 2½ tsp. cornstarch |
| 2½ cups whipping cream |
| For the batter: |
| ½ cup plus 1 tsp. softened butter |
| ¾ cup sugar |
| 4 egg yolks |
| 1 egg |
| Pinch of salt |
| ½ tsp. vanilla |
| 2 tsp. baking powder |
| 1¼ cups flour |
| 2 tbs. milk |
| For the meringue: |
| 4 egg whites |
| 1¼ cups plus 1 tbs. sugar |
| For sprinkling: |
| ½ cup sliced almonds |

To prepare the filling, mix the
lemon rind with the lemon
juice and add water to make ½
cup. Mix the juice with the sugar
and bring to a boil. Stir the cornstarch with 3 tablespoons of cold
water, stir into the lemon juice
and bring to a boil again. •
Cover the cooled lemon cream
and chill over night. • To make
the batter, cream the butter. Drizzle in the sugar a little at a time.
Add the egg yolks, the whole
egg, salt and vanilla. Mix the
baking powder with the flour and
stir in with the milk. • To make

the meringue beat the egg whites
until stiff, drizzling in the sugar a
little at a time. • Preheat the
oven to 350°. If possible butter
the bottoms of two springform
pans and fill each with half of the
batter. • Spread the meringue on
the layers up to the edge of the
pan. Sprinkle with the sliced almonds. • Bake the layers 25
minutes on the middle rack of
the oven. (If only one springform
pan is available bake the layers
in succession.) Cool on a cake
rack. • To make the cream whip
the cream until very stiff and fold
into the lemon cream. Set one
cake layer on a platter and
spread with two-thirds of the
cream. Set the second layer on
top and press down slightly.
Thickly cover the sides with the
rest of the cream. • Decorate and
allow the cake to stand a good 2
hours. It tastes good even the
second day if it has been kept
cool.

## Kiwi Cake

### Somewhat expensive

Preparation time: 20 minutes
Baking time: 30 minutes

Ingredients for a 10-inch
springform pan

For the cake:

6 eggs

Pinch of salt

1 cup sugar

¾ cup plus 1 tbs. flour

⅓ cup plus 1 tbs. cornstarch

1 cup powdered chocolate

1 tsp. baking powder

⅓ cup bread crumbs

For the filling and frosting:

2½ tsp. gelatin

4-5 kiwis

½ cup powdered sugar

2 tsp. sugar

1 tsp. vanilla

2 cups whipping cream

¼ cup sliced almonds

3 tbs. rum

**P**reheat the oven to 350°. •
Separate the eggs. Beat the
egg whites with the salt until
creamy. Drizzle in ½ cup sugar
and beat until very stiff. • Beat
the egg yolks with 2 tablespoons
water and the remaining sugar.
Place the egg whites on the yolk
mixture. Mix the flour with the
cornstarch, powdered chocolate
and baking powder. Sift over the
egg whites and fold into the yolk
mixture with a spatula. • Butter
the bottom of the springform pan
and sprinkle with the bread
crumbs. Spread the batter in the
pan and bake 30 minutes on the
middle rack. • Remove the
sponge cake from the pan and
let stand 24 hours before cutting.
• To make the cream dissolve the
gelatin in a little cold water. Peel
the kiwis, reserving 1 kiwi for
garnish. • Chop the kiwis or

puree in a food processor. Mix
the powdered sugar with the fruit
puree. Whip the cream with the
sugar and vanilla until stiff. Warm
the gelatin over low heat and
gradually combine with the
whipped cream. Chill one-third
of the cream. Mix the remaining
cream with the fruit puree. •
Toast the almonds in a dry pan.
• Cut the cake into three layers
and sprinkle each layer with the
rum. Spread the kiwi cream on
the bottom and second layer and
stack all three layers. Cover the
entire cake with whipped cream.
Place the remaining vanilla-
cream in a pastry bag with a
flower tip and place small
mounds of cream around the top
of the cake. Sprinkle the cooled
sliced almonds in the center. Cut

the remaining kiwi, quarter the
slices and set on the cream rosettes. • Chill the cake until time
to serve.

# Index